BIG ON FLAVOUR
LOW IN FAT

21-68

By the same author

The Stir Fry Cook
The Combination Microwave Cook*

* with Annette Yates

BIG ON FLAVOUR LOW IN FAT

Caroline Young

RIGHT WAY

Typeset in 11/12pt Swiss by Letterpart Ltd., Reigate, Surrey.

Printed and bound in Great Britain by Cox & Wyman Ltd., Reading, Berkshire.

The *Right Way* series is published by Elliot Right Way Books, Brighton Road, Lower Kingswood, Tadworth, Surrey, KT20 6TD, U.K. For information about our company and the other books we publish, visit our web site at www.right-way.co.uk

CONTENTS

CONTENTS

DEDICATION

My grateful thanks to my long-suffering husband, who manfully tries all the recipes and provides his honest comments, and to my ever-helpful friend and colleague, Annette Yates.

The very striking line drawings are the work of Ann Hamilton, who also lives in our small Norfolk village, and the cover photograph was taken by Norwich photographer Des Adams.

INTRODUCTION

- Do you enjoy good food?

- From a health point of view, are you concerned about the *kind* of food you eat?

- Have you bought any of the low-fat or fat-reduced products now filling a large proportion of the shelves in our food shops?

- Are you concerned about the taste, appearance and cost of those products?

- If you read the product label, do you *really* want to eat the unfamiliar ingredients that are listed? The dextrose monohydrate, the stabilizers, the dried whey, the emulsifiers and the thickeners? Do you know what they are? *Should* we be eating them?

- Do you think you should be cutting back on the amount of fat you are eating?

As you have opened this book, I feel sure you will say yes to at least one of those questions and want to know more.

We are being told from all sides – nutritionists, magazines, health writers, even the Government – that we need to reduce the amount of fat we eat. The current trend of television cookery programmes doesn't offer any help, with the emphasis on entertainment and generous helpings of cream, oil and butter. Supermarkets are packed with ready-to-eat food described as 'low-fat' or 'fat-free' but, after reading the ingredient list, I put them straight back on the shelf.

I unashamedly love good food and, with a varied career working with food, have a great interest in it. I enjoy cooking, sourcing regional and organic foods, exploring local farmers' markets, waiting for foods to be in season (that first asparagus!) and, of course, eating the food we grow in our own garden. Before I started work on this book, I wondered, "Is it possible to eat healthily without losing any of that enjoyment?" Having finished writing the book, I can now confirm that it is.

This is not the latest quick fix, lose weight overnight diet book. It is simply a collection of delicious recipes that just happen to be full of flavour and low in fat, made with fresh ingredients and in generous portions. With a few simple changes in cooking techniques, using naturally low fat foods and exploring a variety of flavourings, I have found you can produce dishes that are extremely appetising yet very good for you.

Why do we use fat?
The fat in food not only prevents it from sticking to the pan, where applicable, but also gives an impression of a rounded, full satisfying flavour and 'mouth appeal'. Think of the taste of full fat Jersey milk and mentally compare it with that of skimmed milk and you will understand what I mean. When you cut down on the fat, you can end up with tasteless food. We all need to eat a small amount of fat, omitting it completely from some recipes is quite possible but the end result may disappoint you. By using just a tiny, measured (with proper measuring spoons or with an oil spray) amount of good quality fat – I use olive oil – the recipe is improved immensely.

How much fat should we eat?
The Government-recommended amount for women is 70g per day, for men 95g. It can easily add up: just one

measured tablespoon of oil is 19g, one ounce of Cheddar cheese 10g and the average cheeseburger contains 26g of fat. With each of the recipes in this book I have given the approximate fat count per serving. Ingredients such as vegetables and fruit are virtually fat free and, as such, do not need to be weighed accurately. To keep to the fat count you do need to buy meat, fish and poultry at the weight given and you must use a set of graduated measuring spoons to measure oil, not just any spoon out of the drawer.

Tasty and attractive!

This selection of recipes is anything but tasteless! They look great on the plate, with lots of colourful ingredients in generous amounts and simply bursting with flavour. Cooking and eating should be relaxed and fun. Most of these recipes are great for informal eating in the garden or in front of the television. I serve many of them in bowls, either colourful pottery pasta bowls or some shallow old-fashioned soup plates that are now coming back into fashion thanks to trendy restaurants. One thing I do think is important is to warm the plates or bowls before adding the food, either in a warm oven or in a bowl of very hot, clean water.

The choice of ingredients

I have used lots of fresh herbs, which is one of my favourite ways to add both flavour and colour to a simple dish. They are easy to grow on the smallest window sill, or you can buy those sold in pots and cut them as needed. Alternatively, keep some packets of frozen herbs in the freezer but, please, never resort to using the tasteless dried variety.

I have used well-known flavourings such as soy sauce, fresh root ginger and lots of fresh lemon. A squeeze of fresh lemon juice can work wonders to brighten the taste of a bland food, and lemons will keep for days in the refrigerator.

I always use freshly milled crunchy sea salt crystals and black peppercorns; their flavour really makes a difference to a dish. You can buy inexpensive and ready filled mills for grinding, which you can easily refill when empty, in all supermarkets.

I have also explored using other ingredients you may not be so familiar with, such as sun-dried tomatoes, balsamic vinegar and tamarind paste. To prevent you ending up with half used jars of ingredients in the fridge, I have listed them in the index with the other recipes they are used in. One recipe will have a description of the ingredient and other suggestions for using it.

We are able to buy a tremendous variety of foods, so, instead of spending your money on packaged food, why not spend it on food that tastes delicious naturally and really makes a difference to how you feel? Most fresh foods can be bought, at a price, all the year round but will have travelled many miles to get to our shops. Far better to choose foods in season, preferably locally grown, as they will be fresh, crisp, and have far more flavour (as well as supporting our national farming industry). Try organic vegetables and fruits; they usually contain less water than conventionally grown produce so that their nutritional content is more concentrated, making them taste naturally sweeter and have higher vitamin levels.

The choice of equipment
All the recipes are easy to follow and quick to prepare. Most of them can be on the plate in less than thirty minutes. To reduce the amount of fat needed I use a generous-sized wok and fry-pan with a top quality non-stick finish. Buy the best you can afford, take care of them and they will last for many years. Lids are handy but not essential; you can always improvise with a double sheet of cooking foil if the food needs to be covered at any time. The sheer size of a wok makes it a very versatile piece of equipment. I use mine for cooking pasta, soups and sauces as well as for stir-frying.

A ridged non-stick griddle will produce those attractive browned markings on food but is not essential. You can buy oil-sprays ready to use but I prefer a pump-spray bottle (look for them in kitchen gadget departments) which I can fill with the oil of my own choice. Many of the recipes can be cooked in the microwave (the methods are given in *italics*) and some can be barbecued.

A helping hand for American cooks
Unlike cookbooks with recipes for items such as cakes, which require very precise weighing and measuring of ingredients to ensure success, this book has no such problem. Only the ingredients which contain fat (meat, fish and poultry) must be weighed and these are sold in the USA by weight. You will also need a set of measuring spoons and a calibrated jug with ounces, as well as cup measures for measuring liquids. I have found that many canned foods in the USA are labelled both in grams and ounces. If not, 400g is 14 ounces, 200g is 7 ounces. When a recipe needs stock, use a vegetable or chicken stock cube dissolved in boiling water or, where appropriate, canned consommé.

Vegetables and fruit are sold by weight but one or two names may be confusing. Aubergines are eggplants, courgettes are zucchini and chickpeas may be labelled garbanzo beans. The peppery herb rocket is also called arugula.

With modern transportation methods, most foods can be found in supermarkets all over the world all the year round. Sadly, this blurs the pleasure of eating seasonally and enjoying foods in the country in which they are grown but it does mean most cookbooks can now be used internationally.

So why not dip in and try a recipe or two?
I guarantee you will be surprised – by the flavour, appearance and the size of the portions of all the recipes.

Oh, by the way, I was delighted to find I lost over ten kilos in weight writing this book, not something I usually expect testing recipes!

Caroline Young

1
SOUPS

CHILLED COURGETTE SOUP

A bowl of icy cool, creamy soup makes a very pleasant start to a summer meal. This pale green blend of courgette and yogurt looks very appetising served in chilled glass bowls.

The recipe makes four portions and may be kept in the refrigerator for up to 24 hours.

Serves 4

Approximately 3g of fat per serving

225g/8 oz small courgettes
300ml/½ pint well-flavoured vegetable stock
finely grated rind and juice of 1 lemon
600ml/1 pint natural low fat yogurt
2 tbsp finely chopped fresh mint
freshly milled salt and black pepper
4 tbsp finely chopped fresh chives

1. Trim the courgettes and slice into a pan. Add the stock and bring just to the boil. Cover the pan and cook over a low heat for about 5 minutes or until the courgettes are very soft. Leave until cool.

2. Put the courgettes, stock, lemon rind and juice, and the yogurt into a processor and buzz until smooth.

3. Pour the soup into a bowl and stir in the mint. Cover and refrigerate for at least 3 hours until well chilled.

4. To serve, season to taste, ladle into chilled bowls and sprinkle the chives on top.

MANHATTAN CLAM CHOWDER

Clams are tiny, sweet shellfish and are the main ingredient of Clam Chowder. A chowder is a hearty main dish soup and both France and America have their versions. More than once, I have sat at an American dinner table and listened to heated arguments about the merits of Manhattan Clam Chowder over the New England version. The latter is creamy in colour and richness and is served with tiny plain biscuits called Pilot Crackers while the New York chowder has a tomato base. Which is better? It all depends on where you come from! Unfortunately, the New England Chowder has no place in a cookbook dedicated to lowering the amount of fat in the recipes but this version of Manhattan Clam Chowder you can enjoy with impunity.

Serves 2

Approximately 4.5g of fat per serving

1 slice (25g/1 oz) smoked back bacon
1 small onion
1 medium carrot
2 stalks celery
290g can baby clams in brine
1 large baking potato, about 250g/8 oz
1 tbsp fresh thyme leaves
1 tbsp finely chopped fresh parsley
450ml/¾ pint fish or vegetable stock
200g can chopped tomatoes
2 tbsp dry white vermouth
Tabasco sauce
freshly milled salt and black pepper

1. Finely chop the bacon, discarding any rind. Peel and finely chop the onion. Peel and dice the carrot. Trim and thinly slice the celery. Tip the clams into a strainer, briefly rinse under cold water and leave to drain. Peel the potato and cut into 1cm (½ in) cubes.

2. Put the bacon into a large non-stick pan (I use a wok) and cook, stirring, until it begins to crisp. Add the onion, carrot and celery and cook for 2-3 minutes. Stir in the thyme and half the parsley.

3. Add the stock, tomatoes and potato, stir well and bring to the boil.

4. Cover and cook over medium heat for about 10 minutes or until the potato is just tender.

5. Add the clams, vermouth, and the Tabasco and seasoning to taste. Heat to serving temperature.

6. Spoon into warmed bowls and serve with the remaining parsley sprinkled over the top.

FISH CHOWDER

This is just the soup for a chilly day, really chunky and rich in flavour with lots of vegetables and fish. Serve with some warm granary bread for a good meal.

I have suggested using leeks and courgettes but onion and carrots, even some diced potato, would be equally good. Add curry paste to your taste. The dry milk powder, a useful thing to have in the cupboard, adds richness but not fat to the soup.

Serves 2

Approximately 3.5g of fat per serving

2 small leeks – about 150g/5½ oz
2 small courgettes – about 150g/5½ oz
2 celery stalks
225g/8 oz firm white fish such as cod, haddock or coley
2 tsp curry paste
1 tsp tomato purée
450ml/15 fl oz hot fish or vegetable stock
55g/2 oz sweetcorn, canned or frozen
2 tbsp skimmed milk powder
a dash of dry sherry
freshly milled salt and black pepper

1. Trim the leeks, cut in half lengthways and wash under running water to remove any grit. Drain, then thinly slice. Trim the courgettes and celery and cut into thin slices. Remove and discard any skin or bones from the fish and cut it into bite-sized pieces.

2. Put all the vegetables into a large non-stick pan (or wok). Stir the curry paste and tomato purée into the stock and add to the vegetables.

3.   Bring to the boil, then reduce the heat to low, cover the pan and cook gently for about 10 minutes or until the vegetables are just tender.

4.   Stir in the fish and sweetcorn. Cover and cook over low heat for about 5 minutes or until the fish is opaque.

5.   Stir the milk powder into 2 tbsp cold water and add with the sherry plus seasoning to taste. Heat gently until piping hot but do not allow to boil as this will spoil the texture.

MICROWAVE METHOD (See page 215.)

1.   Trim the leeks, cut in half lengthways and wash under running water to remove any grit. Drain, then thinly slice. Trim the courgettes and celery and cut into thin slices. Remove and discard any skin or bones from the fish and cut into bite-size pieces.

2.   Put all the vegetables into a large casserole. Stir the curry paste and tomato purée into the HOT stock and add to the vegetables.

3.   Cook on HIGH for 4-5 minutes, stirring once, or until the stock just comes to the boil. Cover with a vented lid and cook on MEDIUM-HIGH for 6-8 minutes, stirring once, or until the vegetables are just tender.

4.   Stir in the fish and sweetcorn. Replace the lid and cook on MEDIUM for about 4 minutes or until the fish is opaque.

5.   Stir the milk powder into 2 tbsp cold water and add with the sherry plus seasoning to taste. Stir well, then cook on MEDIUM-HIGH for 1 minute or until piping hot. Do not allow to boil.

GAZPACHO

There are numerous versions of this well-known chilled soup but this is my favourite. Roasted garlic (see page 201) gives the soup a mellow flavour but if you haven't any handy, use one fresh garlic clove, peeled and crushed, instead. The bread gives the soup texture; it only needs a light toasting to dry it slightly. This recipe makes 4 portions but the soup will keep for 2 days in the refrigerator.

Serve the soup well chilled, even pop the serving bowls in the fridge to chill as well. If wished, you could add a couple of ice cubes to each portion just before serving. The addition of some cooked shrimps would make it into a light meal.

Serves 4

Approximately 1.5g of fat per serving

1 red and 1 yellow pepper
½ cucumber
6 spring onions
1 thick slice white bread
6 sun-dried tomato pieces (the dry-packed variety)
2 roasted garlic cloves
600ml/1 pint cool, well-flavoured vegetable stock
330ml can vegetable juice
3 tbsp red wine vinegar
freshly milled salt and black pepper
1 tbsp finely chopped fresh parsley

1. Halve the peppers, removing the stem, any white pith and the seeds. Cut the flesh into small cubes and place in a large bowl. Peel the cucumber (easiest with a swivel potato peeler) and cut in half lengthways. Scoop out and discard the seeds, then cut the flesh into small cubes and add to the bowl. Trim and thinly slice the onions and add to the bowl. Stir thoroughly to mix the vegetables.

2. Lightly toast the bread. Put the tomatoes into a small bowl and cover with boiling water.

3. Put the bread into a processor and buzz to coarse crumbs. Add about one-third of the vegetables, the roasted or crushed garlic and the stock. Buzz to a coarse purée, then tip back into the bowl.

4. Drain and chop the tomatoes and add to the bowl with the vegetable juice, and vinegar. Stir well and season to taste.

5. Cover and chill for at least 3 hours. Just before serving stir in the parsley.

WHITE BEAN AND CABBAGE SOUP

This is a recipe I turn to when I feel I have been over-eating high fat foods and need to feel virtuous but still eat well. Beans are a good source of low-fat protein and, combined with fresh vegetables, make a well-balanced and satisfying dish. Just add some warm granary bread and you will feel very well fed. If you can only find 400g cans of beans, use half and tip the remainder into a storage container and refrigerate (do not leave in the can). Use (within 24 hours) in a salad or add some lemon juice, chopped fresh herbs such as chives, plus seasoning, and mash with a fork to make a sandwich filling similar to hummus but far lower in fat (about 1g).

Serves 2

Approximately 5g of fat per serving

1 small onion
1 large carrot
1 garlic clove
225g/8 oz wedge of white cabbage
200g can cannellini beans
oil spray
600ml/1 pint vegetable stock
200g can chopped tomatoes
1 tbsp finely chopped fresh parsley
freshly milled salt and pepper
1 tbsp freshly grated Parmesan cheese

1. Peel and finely chop the onion. Peel the carrot and cut into small cubes. Peel and crush the garlic. Cut out the thick stem and ribs of the cabbage and finely shred the leaves. Tip the beans into a strainer, rinse under cold water, then leave to drain.

2. Lightly spray a large non-stick pan (such as a wok) with oil and add the onion and carrot. Cover and cook over medium heat, stirring, for a few minutes or until the onion is soft.

3. Add the garlic, stock, tomatoes, cabbage and beans. Bring just to the boil, then cover and cook over a low heat for 10 minutes or until the vegetables are tender.

4. Stir in the parsley and season to taste.

5. Ladle into warm bowls and sprinkle the Parmesan cheese on top.

MICROWAVE METHOD (See page 215.)

1. *Peel and finely chop the onion. Peel the carrot and cut into small cubes. Peel and crush the garlic. Cut out the thick stem and ribs of the cabbage and finely shred the leaves. Tip the beans into a strainer, rinse under cold water, then leave to drain.*

2. *Put the onion and carrot into a large casserole and lightly spray with oil. Cover and cook on HIGH for 1-2 minutes or until the onion is soft.*

3. *Add the garlic, HOT stock, tomatoes, cabbage and beans. Cook on HIGH for 2-3 minutes or until the stock just comes to the boil. Cover with a vented lid and cook on MEDIUM-HIGH for about 6 minutes, stirring once, or until the vegetables are tender.*

4. *Stir in the parsley and season to taste.*

5. *Ladle into warm bowls and sprinkle the Parmesan cheese on top.*

BUTTERBEAN AND LEMON SOUP

I would serve this smooth and creamy soup as a starter before a fairly light main dish, such as a vegetable stir fry, or even for lunch with a hearty sandwich.

If you have some roasted garlic to hand (see page 201), using it in this recipe in place of fresh garlic will give a subtle mellow flavour. Alternatively, cook the fresh garlic cloves in half the stock, covered and over low heat, for a few minutes before adding the beans in step 2. However, if you are really short of time, the recipe is still very good using fresh crushed garlic.

Using only half the measured liquid in a soup recipe in the initial cooking, before buzzing in a processor, gives a much smoother texture. Dried skimmed milk powder adds a rich creamy taste and texture to a soup with very little additional fat.

Serves 2

Approximately 1.5g of fat per serving

400g can butterbeans
1 garlic clove
finely grated rind and juice of 1 large lemon
600ml/1 pint vegetable stock
2 tbsp dried skimmed milk powder
freshly milled salt and black pepper
2 tbsp finely chopped fresh chives

1. Tip the beans into a sieve and rinse under cold water. Peel and crush the garlic (see above).

2. Put the beans, garlic, lemon rind and juice and HALF the stock into a non-stick pan. Bring just to the boil, then cover and cook over medium heat for 5 minutes. Cool slightly.

3. Spoon the soup into a processor, add the milk powder and buzz until smooth. Return to the pan and stir in the remaining stock.

4. Season to taste and gently heat to serving temperature. Do not allow the soup to boil as this will spoil the texture.

5. Spoon into warm bowls and sprinkle the chives on top.

MICROWAVE METHOD (See page 215.)

1. Tip the beans into a sieve and rinse under cold water. Peel and crush the garlic (see opposite).

2. Put the beans, garlic, lemon rind and juice and HALF the HOT stock into a casserole. Cover with a vented lid and cook on HIGH for 2-3 minutes or until the liquid just comes to the boil. Cool slightly.

3. Spoon the soup into a processor, add the milk and buzz until smooth. Return to the casserole and stir in the remaining stock.

4. Season to taste and heat, uncovered, on MEDIUM-HIGH for 2-3 minutes, stirring once, or until at serving temperature. Do not allow to boil. Serve as above.

ICED CUCUMBER SOUP WITH TOMATO SALSA

On a hot day a bowl of cool soup flavoured with lots of fresh garden herbs makes a delicious start to a meal.

Be sure to chill the soup well before serving. The soup can be refrigerated for up to 48 hours. Use natural yogurt made with full fat milk; the soup will not taste as creamy if made with lower fat varieties. If preferred, a spoonful of pesto sauce (see page 192) in place of the salsa would taste equally good.

Makes about 1 litre/1¾ pints

Serves 4

Approximately 2.6g of fat per serving

1 large cucumber
250g/9 oz full fat natural yogurt
300ml/½ pint cool, well-flavoured vegetable or
   chicken stock
4 tbsp chopped mint
4 tbsp chopped chives
2 tbsp white wine vinegar
1 large ripe tomato
1 small red onion
2-3 tsp red wine vinegar
1 tsp olive oil
freshly milled salt and black pepper

1. Peel the cucumber, cut in half lengthways and scoop out the seeds (a serrated-edged spoon is handy for this).

2. Roughly chop the cucumber and put into a processor or blender with the yogurt, stock, herbs and white wine vinegar. Buzz until very smooth.

3. Tip into a bowl, cover and refrigerate for several hours (or overnight) until very cold.

4. To make the salsa, cover the tomato with boiling water and leave to stand for a few minutes. Drain and slip off the skin. Cut into quarters, remove and discard the stem, seeds and core. Chop the flesh into tiny cubes and place in a bowl. Peel the onion, finely chop and add to the bowl. Stir in the red wine vinegar and olive oil, cover and chill with the soup.

5. To serve, stir the soup, adding seasoning to taste. Season the salsa.

6. Spoon into chilled soup bowls and top each serving with a spoonful of salsa.

2
PASTA

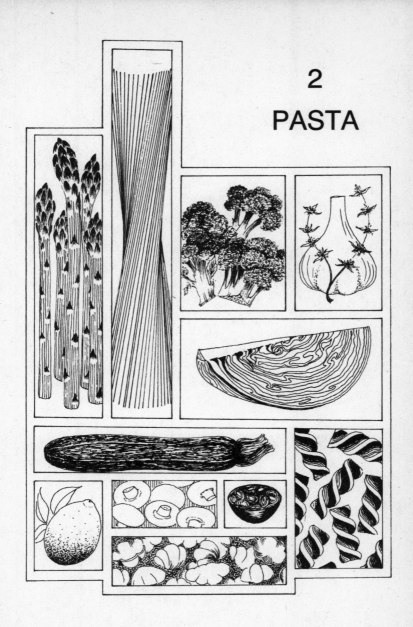

TERIYAKI VEGETABLES

Fast food in a bowl.

Serves 2

Approximately 2g of fat per serving

2 portions of rice noodles
400g can bean sprouts
several spring onions
1 Little Gem lettuce or a handful of fresh spinach
** leaves**
1 clove garlic
2 tsp clear honey or maple syrup
3 tbsp soy sauce
1 tbsp finely chopped or grated root ginger
2 tbsp dry sherry or vegetable stock
freshly milled salt and black pepper

1. Cook the noodles to packet directions.

2. Tip the bean sprouts into a strainer to drain. Trim
    and slice the spring onions. Roughly shred the
    lettuce or spinach. Peel and crush the garlic.

3. Spoon the honey (or maple syrup), soy sauce,
    ginger and sherry (or stock) into a non-stick wok.
    Add the spring onions, bean sprouts and lettuce
    (or spinach). Cook over high heat, stirring con-
    stantly, until the vegetables are just wilted.

4. Drain the noodles and add to the wok with season-
    ing to taste. Gently toss together and serve imme-
    diately.

PASTA AND CHICKPEA SALAD

I like to have a substantial pasta or grain salad in the fridge during the warmer months, to dip into when I would rather be in the garden than cooking in the kitchen. In fact, they seem to improve with keeping (up to 48 hours) as the flavours develop and become absorbed. I would recommend spooning the salad into bowls an hour before you want to eat it, as the flavour is so much better at room temperature. If you must add some cheese, 30g of salty ewe's milk Feta adds up to 7g of fat, 30g of pungent goat's cheese 4.5g of fat.

Pasta, rice, grains and beans all absorb flavours better if they are combined hot. Adding the chickpeas to the pasta for a couple of minutes will do the trick.

Serves 4

Approximately 7g of fat per serving

4 ripe plum tomatoes
1 bunch spring onions
2 garlic cloves
4 tbsp orange or English apple juice
finely grated rind and juice of 1 large lemon
1 tbsp olive oil
1 tbsp clear honey
1 tbsp whole grain mustard
freshly milled salt and black pepper
2 tbsp finely chopped fresh mint
375g can chickpeas
175g/6 oz pasta shapes such as penne
extra finely chopped fresh mint to garnish

1. Cover the tomatoes with boiling water and leave to stand for a few minutes. Drain and slice off the stem ends. Slip off the skins and cut each tomato in half. Scoop out and discard the seeds, then roughly chop the flesh. Trim the spring onions and thinly slice.

2. Peel the garlic and crush into a serving bowl. Add the orange (or apple) juice, lemon rind and juice, oil, honey and mustard, and whisk until thoroughly combined. Add seasoning to taste and the chopped mint.

3. Drain the chickpeas and rinse under cold water. Cook the pasta to packet directions, adding the drained chickpeas for the last 2-3 minutes.

4. Drain the pasta and chickpeas thoroughly, tip into the bowl of dressing and stir to combine.

5. Leave the pasta and chickpeas to cool to room temperature, then gently stir in the tomatoes and spring onions and check to see if you need to add any more seasoning. Just before serving, give the salad a good stir.

6. Serve with extra mint sprinkled on top, plus the crumbled cheese if using.

FUSILLI WITH BROCCOLI AND RED PEPPER

This very quickly cooked pasta dish has a bright fresh flavour. If wished add a few stoned and sliced black olives but six (40g) will add 3.5g of fat to each serving. Originating in Tunisia, harissa is a pungent fiery sauce made with hot chillies and spices; it is the traditional accompaniment for couscous. Once found only in ethnic markets it is now in most food stores, packed in tiny jars. It has a wonderful flavour but should be used with discretion until you develop a taste for it. Alternatively add a teaspoon or so of chilli sauce.

Serves 2

Approximately 5g of fat per serving

1 medium-sized head of broccoli
1 red pepper
2 garlic cloves
finely grated rind and juice of 1 lemon
1 tbsp sun-dried tomato paste
¼-½ tsp harissa sauce
150ml/¼ pint vegetable stock
175g/6 oz fusilli (twists) pasta
freshly milled salt and black pepper

1. Trim the broccoli, discarding any thick stems and break the florets into bite-sized pieces. Cut the pepper in half lengthways. Remove and discard the stem, seeds and any white pith, then cut the flesh into thin strips. Peel and crush the garlic. Add the lemon rind and juice, the tomato paste and harissa to the stock and stir to combine.

2. Bring a large pan of water to the boil (I use my wok), add a good pinch of salt and stir in the pasta. Cook for HALF the time instructed on the packet, then stir in the broccoli, bring back to the boil and continue to cook for the remaining time. Tip into a colander and leave to drain.

3. While the pasta is cooking put the stock mixture, the garlic and red pepper into a pan, bring to the boil, then reduce the heat and cook, covered, just until the pepper is soft.

4. Return the drained pasta and broccoli to the large pan (wok), add the pepper mixture and gently stir to combine.

5. Season to taste, then spoon into warmed bowls and serve immediately.

SPAGHETTI WITH FRESH VEGETABLE AND HERB SAUCE

Say spaghetti sauce and you probably think of a thick tomato sauce with, or without, meat. This recipe is totally different. Think of a creamy sauce flavoured with fresh herbs, folded into the hot pasta and topped with a colourful combination of lightly cooked vegetables – deliciously different. Serve with a crunchy salad of sliced Romaine or Cos lettuce, tossed with the dressing of your choice, plus some good warm bread.

Buy fresh young broad beans in season or, if not available, use 115g/4 oz frozen petit pois (please don't use frozen broad beans as they have unpleasant thick skins). Courgettes are in the shops all the year round but do buy the smallest you can find and, if possible, in more than one colour (they come in shades of green and yellow).

Serves 2

Approximately 7g of fat per serving

450g/1 lb young broad beans in the pods
225g/8 oz cherry tomatoes
225g/8 oz young courgettes
200g/7 oz 'virtually fat-free' fromage frais
2 tbsp finely chopped fresh mint
4 tbsp finely chopped fresh chives
freshly milled salt and black pepper
8 black olives in brine
225g/8 oz spaghetti
oil spray

1. Shell the broad beans. Cut each tomato in half. Trim the courgettes and cut across into thin slices.

2. Spoon the fromage frais into a bowl and stir in the herbs. Season to taste.

3. Bring a large pan (I use a wok) of boiling, salted water to the boil and add the spaghetti. Cook for the time given on the packet, adding the beans for the last 2-3 minutes.

4. Meanwhile, heat a non-stick fry-pan and lightly spray with oil. Add the courgettes and cook, stirring, until golden brown on both sides and just tender. Stir in the tomatoes and olives and cook for another couple of minutes to heat through.

5. Drain the spaghetti and beans, reserving a little of the cooking water. Tip the pasta and beans back into the pan.

6. If the fromage frais is rather thick, stir in a spoonful or so of the pasta water. You are aiming for a thick cream consistency. Tip the sauce into the pasta and lightly blend together with two forks.

7. Pile into warmed bowls (or plates), spoon the vegetables on top and serve immediately.

PENNE WITH ASPARAGUS

This is a recipe to enjoy in the early summer when English asparagus comes into season. The really big fat spears are so special they should simply be steamed or cooked in the microwave until just tender and dressed very lightly with a sprinkling of excellent virgin olive oil and crunchy sea salt. For this recipe choose medium-thick spears that are firm, smooth and bright green with tightly packed tips – the indication that the asparagus is freshly picked and in prime condition. Always tear basil leaves, as chopping with a knife can discolour them.

Serves 2

Approximately 7.5g of fat per serving

3 ripe plum tomatoes
225g/8 oz asparagus spears
175g/6 oz penne pasta
300ml/½ pint chicken or vegetable stock
2 tbsp dry white vermouth
freshly milled salt and black pepper
15g (½ oz) basil leaves
2 tbsp freshly grated Parmesan cheese

1.	Cover the tomatoes with boiling water and leave to stand for 4-5 minutes. Drain, cut out the stem ends and slip off the skins. Cut into quarters and scoop out and discard the seeds. Cut off any woody, tough ends from the asparagus and cut the stalks into 5cm/2 in pieces.

2.	Cook the pasta to packet directions in a large pan of lightly salted, boiling water until just tender.

3.	Meanwhile, using a large fry-pan bring the stock just to the boil. Add the asparagus and cook over medium heat for 4 minutes. Add the tomatoes and continue to cook for about 3 minutes or until the asparagus is just tender.

4.	Drain the pasta and tip into a large, warmed bowl. Using a slotted spoon, add the asparagus and tomatoes. Cover and keep warm.

5.	Add the vermouth to the stock and bring to the boil, stirring. Allow to boil for about 2 minutes or until slightly reduced. Season to taste.

6.	Add the sauce, roughly torn basil leaves and Parmesan cheese to the pasta and vegetables. Gently toss to combine, then spoon into warm bowls and serve immediately.

CHINESE NOODLES WITH VEGETABLES

This is a good recipe to choose when you feel you have over indulged on high fat foods! With lots of vegetables it is a very satisfying and comforting dish. The technique of stir-frying need not involve cooking in oil. In this recipe I have used a combination of oriental sauces but you could use just a few spoonfuls of well-flavoured stock. I often use this method to cook vegetables quickly for a side dish, such as thinly sliced leeks, cabbage or Brussels sprouts. Cook in a wok for a few minutes until just tender.

I have suggested using Savoy cabbage but Pak Choi or Chinese Leaves would be equally good. I find canned bean sprouts (useful to keep in the cupboard) are smaller than fresh but either is fine. In fact, you could use any combination of vegetables in this recipe. Just cut them to a similar size before starting to cook.

Sesame oil, extracted from sesame seeds, has a delicious nutty flavour and aroma. You will find several kinds in the stores: one lightly coloured and flavoured; a darker toasted sesame oil; and a smoked oil with a richer smoky flavour. Light sesame oil can be used for frying but the darker varieties are usually added at the end of the cooking time as a flavouring.

Serves 2

Approximately 8.5g of fat per serving

**a small wedge of Savoy cabbage or other greens,
see opposite**
2 small carrots
2 small leeks
410g can bean sprouts
2 portions of egg or rice noodles
2 tbsp soy sauce
2 tbsp hoisin sauce
freshly milled salt and black pepper
1 tbsp dark or smoked sesame oil

1. Trim the cabbage, removing and discarding any thick ribs, and cut into thin shreds. You need a couple of good handfuls. Peel the carrots and cut into matchstick-sized pieces or grate on the coarse blade of a grater. Trim the leeks and cut in half lengthways. Thoroughly rinse under cold water and drain well, then cut into thin slices. Drain the bean sprouts.

2. Cook the noodles to packet directions.

3. Preheat a non-stick wok and add the soy and hoisin sauces. Add the cabbage, carrots and leeks and cook, stirring, over medium heat until just tender. Stir in the bean sprouts and cook for 1-2 minutes or until piping hot. Season to taste.

4. Drain the noodles and toss with the sesame oil. Add to the wok, stirring to combine with the vegetables. Spoon into bowls and serve immediately.

NOODLES WITH PEPPER AND CHINESE GREENS

This very quick stir-fry with noodles is the dish I make when I only want a light meal or am in a hurry. If you haven't a fresh green chilli in the fridge, add a little chilli sauce with the soy sauce. Chinese leaves are the most familiar Oriental greens in our shops but if you can find Pak Choi it is excellent in this recipe.

The cooking time is so short it is important to prepare all the ingredients before starting to cook.

Serves 2

Approximately 2.5g of fat per serving

6 spring onions
140g/5 oz Chinese leaves or Pak Choi
1 small red or yellow pepper
1 fresh green chilli
220g can water chestnuts
1 garlic clove
1 tbsp finely chopped or grated fresh root ginger
115g/4 oz medium egg noodles
oil spray
3 tbsp soy sauce
freshly milled salt and black pepper

1. Trim and thickly slice the onions. Trim and thinly shred the Chinese leaves or Pak Choi. Cut the pepper in half, removing and discarding the stem, pith and seeds, then finely slice the flesh. Cut the chilli in half lengthwise, removing and discarding the stem and seeds. Cut the flesh into fine shreds. (Wash your hands after preparing chillies as they can irritate the skin.) Drain the water chestnuts and cut them in half horizontally. Peel and crush the garlic.

2. Cook the noodles to package directions.

3. Preheat a non-stick wok, then spray with oil. Add all the vegetables and cook over high heat, stirring constantly, until they are soft – about 3-4 minutes.

4. Drain the noodles and add to the wok. Sprinkle over the soy sauce and cook, stirring, for 1 minute. Season to taste, then pile in warmed bowls and serve immediately.

FRESH TAGLIATELLE WITH MUSHROOM RAGOUT

This recipe could be made with a selection of the more exotic looking varieties of mushroom now readily available. They certainly look very attractive but for flavour I always go for the brown chestnut mushrooms and, as in this recipe, intensify that flavour by adding just a few dried mushrooms. The distinctive mushroom flavour becomes more concentrated when the fungi are dried. The most prized of these (and most expensive) are ceps but the packs of wild mushrooms often labelled "wild forest mushrooms" are very good value. Cultivated fresh mushrooms are grown in sterilized soil so do not need washing or peeling. Trim the stems and wipe with a soft cloth or paper towel. Sun-dried tomato paste has a higher fat content than the more familiar concentrated purée sold in tubes but has a sweeter more mellow flavour and I prefer to use it in recipes such as this one where the other ingredients are very low in fat.

Serves 2

Approximately 3g of fat per serving

10g/¼ oz dried mushrooms
225g/8 oz chestnut closed cap mushrooms
1 small onion
1 garlic clove
225g/8 oz fresh tagliatelle
150ml/5 fl oz vegetable stock
2 tbsp dry white vermouth
1 tbsp sun-dried tomato paste
1 tbsp fresh thyme leaves
freshly milled salt and black pepper
1 tbsp finely chopped fresh parsley

1. Prepare the dried mushrooms to packet directions, then tip into a sieve to drain.

2. Trim the chestnut mushrooms and cut each one in half. Peel and finely slice the onion. Peel and crush the garlic.

3. Cook the tagliatelle to packet directions.

4. Meanwhile, put the chestnut mushrooms and onion into a non-stick fry-pan and cook, stirring, over a medium-high heat until they begin to brown. Add the garlic, stock, vermouth, tomato paste, thyme and the drained dried mushrooms.

5. Continue to cook, stirring, until the liquids come to the boil and slightly reduce to form a syrupy sauce. Season to taste and stir in the parsley.

6. Drain the pasta and spoon into warmed bowls. Add the mushroom mixture and serve immediately.

PASTA WITH VEGETABLES AND EGGS

Though this recipe is very simple and takes only minutes to make, success does depend on the cooking
times. Make sure you cook the vegetables only until
they are just crisp, they should still have a slight bite to
them. It is also important that the eggs are only lightly
boiled so that, when they are cut, the soft yolk forms a
sauce which flows over the pasta and vegetables.

Serves 2

Approximately 8.5g of fat per serving

8 spring onions
2 small courgettes
115g/4 oz young asparagus spears
175g/6 oz pasta shapes such as twists
2 medium-sized eggs
4 tbsp soy sauce
freshly milled salt and black pepper

1. Trim the spring onions and cut into 5cm/2 in
    pieces. Trim the courgettes and thinly slice. Cut off
    any woody ends from the asparagus and cut the
    stems into 5cm/2 in pieces.

2. Cook the pasta to package instructions.

3. Put the eggs into a pan of boiling water, reduce the
    heat and simmer gently, allowing 3 minutes from
    the time the water comes back to the boil. Remove
    the eggs from the water, place immediately in cold
    water and leave for about 8 minutes.

4. Lightly cook the vegetables in a pan of simmering
    water for about 4 minutes or until just tender. Tip
    into a colander to drain.

5.   Gently tap the egg shells to crack them, then carefully peel away all the shell.

6.   Drain the pasta and return to the pan. Sprinkle over the soy sauce, add the vegetables and gently mix with two spoons. Season to taste.

7.   Spoon the pasta mixture into warmed bowls and top each with an egg. Serve immediately.

MICROWAVE METHOD (See page 215.)

1.   Trim the spring onions and cut into 5cm/2 in pieces. Trim the courgettes and thinly slice. Cut off any woody ends from the asparagus and cut the stems into 5cm/2 in pieces.

2.   Cook the pasta to package instructions.

3.   Put the eggs into a pan of boiling water on the hob, reduce the heat and simmer gently, allowing 3 minutes from the time the water comes back to the boil. Remove the eggs from the water, place immediately in cold water and leave for about 8 minutes.

4.   Place the vegetables in a casserole with 2 tsp water. Cover and cook on HIGH for 5 minutes or until just tender. Drain.

5.   Gently tap the egg shells to crack them, then carefully peel away all the shell.

6.   Drain the pasta and return to the casserole. Sprinkle over the soy sauce, add the vegetables and gently mix with two spoons. Season to taste.

7.   Spoon the pasta mixture into warmed bowls and top each with an egg. Serve immediately.

PASTA WITH MUSHROOM SAUCE

Sometimes I just have to eat something flavoured with cheese! This recipe helps get me over that craving. To prevent myself nibbling on chunks of cheese while I am preparing the ingredients, I grate the whole piece into a freezer bag, then quickly get it into the freezer. When I need some for a recipe, I just tip out the exact amount I need (still frozen) and put the remainder back into the freezer. There is no need to thaw the grated cheese before adding it to a recipe. Use a really mature or smoked Cheddar cheese for maximum flavour impact.

Harissa sauce, made from chillies, herbs and spices, adds a deep warmth to the sauce. If not available, use chilli sauce or powder to taste.

Serves 2

Approximately 13.5g of fat per serving

225g/8 oz closed cup white or chestnut mushrooms
1 garlic clove
2 tbsp tomato purée
2-3 tsp harissa paste
2 tbsp fresh thyme leaves
200ml/7 fl oz semi-skimmed milk
115g/4 oz pasta such as spirals
freshly milled salt and black pepper
55g/2 oz grated mature or smoked Cheddar cheese

1. Trim the mushrooms, wipe with a clean, dry tea-towel and cut into thick slices. Peel and crush the garlic. Stir the tomato purée, harissa and thyme into the milk.

2. Cook the pasta to packet directions.

3. Heat a non-stick fry-pan and add the mushrooms. Cook over high heat, stirring, until the mushrooms are golden brown. Stir in the garlic and the milk mixture and continue to cook, stirring, until the sauce reduces slightly.

4. Drain the pasta and add to the mushroom sauce. Season to taste and lightly stir together.

5. Spoon into a shallow flameproof dish and scatter the cheese evenly over the top. Slip under a hot grill for a few minutes until the cheese has melted and is golden brown.

VERY QUICK PASTA SAUCES

I know that feeling: a long difficult day, a crowded train or a traffic jam, and you get home and are hungry! Instant nourishment is needed. You look in the fridge and inspiration flies out the window.

Here are three very quick, simple pasta sauces, made with ingredients you probably have in the refrigerator and cupboard. For ravenous appetites increase the amount of pasta to 225g/8 oz and add on an extra 0.5g of fat per serving. I cook the pasta in a non-stick wok; when cooked, tip it into a colander to drain; and then cook the remaining ingredients in the (unwashed) wok. Its generous size makes it easy to lightly toss the cooked ingredients together without breaking up the pasta, plus you have only one pan to wash!

FRESH TOMATO SAUCE

Serves 2   *Approximately 2g of fat per serving*

175g/6 oz pasta
3-4 tomatoes or a handful of cherry tomatoes
a generous amount of finely chopped herbs, such
   as parsley or chives, fresh or frozen
50ml/2 fl oz vegetable or chicken stock
2 tbsp tomato purée
freshly milled salt and black pepper

1.   Cook the pasta to packet directions in a generous amount of lightly salted boiling water.

2.   Cut the tomatoes into thin wedges or the cherry tomatoes in half. Chop the herbs.

3.   Tip the cooked pasta into a colander to drain.

4.   Place the stock and tomato purée into the pan (no need to wash it first) and bring to the boil, stirring to combine. Stir in the tomatoes, herbs, pasta and seasoning to taste. Lightly toss together and serve immediately.

RED PEPPER AND SUN-DRIED TOMATO SAUCE

Serves 2   *Approximately 4.5g of fat per serving*

175g/6 oz pasta
4-5 dry-packed sun-dried tomatoes
1 red, yellow or orange pepper
1 tsp olive oil
1 tsp clear honey
1 tbsp balsamic vinegar
freshly milled salt and black pepper

1.   Cook the pasta in a generous amount of lightly salted water to packet directions.

2.   Cut the sun-dried tomatoes into thin slivers and add to the pasta for the last minute of the cooking time. Cut the pepper into quarters and remove all the seeds and any white pith. Cut the flesh into fine shreds.

3.   Spoon a little of the cooking water into a bowl, then tip the cooked pasta and tomatoes into a colander to drain.

4.   Put the oil, pepper shreds and honey into the pan (no need to wash it first) and cook, stirring, for a minute or two or until the pepper is soft. Tip the drained pasta into the wok and sprinkle with the vinegar. Add seasoning to taste and lightly toss together. If the mixture is a little dry add a spoonful or two of the cooking liquid. Serve immediately.

TUNA AND LEMON SAUCE

Serves 2

Approximately 7g of fat per serving

175g/6 oz pasta
200g can tuna steaks in brine
finely grated rind and juice of 1 large lemon
a generous amount of finely chopped fresh or
**   frozen chives**
2 tsp olive oil
freshly milled salt and black pepper

1. Cook the pasta in a generous amount of lightly salted water to packet directions.

2. Drain the tuna and break up into chunks with a fork.

3. Tip the cooked pasta into a colander to drain.

4. Place the tuna, lemon rind and juice, the chives and oil into the pan (no need to wash it first) and heat, stirring, very briefly just to warm through. Add the drained pasta with seasoning to taste and lightly toss to combine.

5. Serve immediately.

3

RICE
GRAINS
&
BEANS

SPICED COUSCOUS WITH DRIED FRUITS

Dried fruits add colour and sweetness to this quick dish which I serve with grilled meats or chicken. I often double the quantities, serve half, then cover and chill the remainder. The next day I add some fresh lemon juice or a dash of rice vinegar, stir through with a fork and serve at room temperature, either just with some bread or with cold meats and salad.

Serves 2

Approximately 8g of fat per serving

50g/2 oz ready-to-eat dried apricots
4 tbsp orange juice
25g/1 oz dried cherries, cranberries or currants
350ml/12 fl oz vegetable stock
a pinch of ground cinnamon
a pinch of ground coriander
1 tbsp grated or finely chopped fresh root ginger
115g/4 oz couscous
freshly milled salt and black pepper
25g/1 oz toasted flaked almonds

1. Using scissors, roughly cut the apricots into a serving bowl. Stir in the orange juice and dried cherries (cranberries or currants). Leave to soak for about 10 minutes.

2. Meanwhile, pour the stock into a saucepan, stir in the cinnamon, coriander and ginger and bring to the boil. Add the couscous, stir well, cover and leave to stand 10 minutes.

3. Tip the couscous into the serving bowl with the soaked fruits. Add seasoning to taste and lightly stir with a fork until combined.

4. Serve with the almonds scattered over the top.

OVEN BAKED RICE

When cooking other dishes in the oven, if rice is a suitable accompaniment, I utilize the oven space by cooking Oven Baked Rice at the same time (see the Oven Baked Chicken recipe on page 153). I have added peas but they could equally be frozen corn, sliced green beans or mixed vegetables.

Serves 2

Approximately 8g of fat per serving

1 medium-sized onion
1 garlic clove (optional)
2 tsp olive oil
115g/4 oz long grain white rice
350ml/12 fl oz hot chicken or vegetable stock
75g/3 oz frozen peas
freshly milled salt and black pepper
1 tbsp finely chopped fresh parsley or chives
  (optional)

1. Thirty minutes before serving: peel and finely chop the onion. Peel and crush the garlic (if using). Put the onion and oil into an ovenproof casserole and stir to combine.

2. Cover and put into the hot oven (about 190°C/gas mark 5) and cook for 5 minutes.

3. Add the garlic and rice, stirring to coat them with the oil, then stir in the hot stock.

4.   Cover and return to the oven. Cook for 15-20 minutes or until the rice has absorbed all the stock and is tender to the bite.

5.   Meanwhile, put the peas into a strainer and rinse under very hot water until thawed. Stir into the cooked rice and return to the oven for 5 minutes.

6.   To serve, add seasoning to taste and the chopped herbs (if using) and stir through with a fork.

MICROWAVE METHOD (See page 215.)

1.   *Fifteen minutes before serving: peel and finely chop the onion. Peel and crush the garlic (if using).*

2.   *Put the onion and oil into a casserole, cover and cook for 2-3 minutes on HIGH, or until the onion is soft.*

3.   *Add the garlic and rice, stirring to coat them with the oil, then stir in the HOT stock.*

4.   *Cook, uncovered, for about 8 minutes on HIGH.*

5.   *Meanwhile, put the peas into a strainer and rinse under very hot water until thawed. Stir in to the rice and continue to cook, uncovered, for 2 minutes, or until the rice has absorbed all the stock. Cover and leave to stand for 2-3 minutes.*

6.   *Complete the recipe as above.*

SPICED BASMATI RICE

Basmati rice already has a wonderful aroma and flavour which can be enhanced even further with the addition of spicy seeds and some fresh coriander. It goes well with many of the recipes in this book, especially Marinated Lamb with Honey and Thyme Sauce (page 150) and Chicken with Balsamic Vinegar and Orange Sauce (page 168).

Some manufacturers recommend rinsing and soaking Basmati rice before cooking so check the packet instructions. Rinsing removes any rice flour clinging to the grains, giving a lighter texture to the cooked dish.

Serves 2

Approximately 4g of fat per serving

175g/6 oz white Basmati rice
450ml/15 fl oz chicken or vegetable stock
½ tsp coriander seeds
½ tsp cumin seeds
½ tsp black mustard seeds
½ cinnamon stick
2 tbsp finely chopped fresh coriander

1.   Put the rice into a pan with the stock, coriander, cumin and mustard seeds and cinnamon.

2.   Bring to the boil, then cover and reduce the heat to low. Cook until the rice has absorbed the stock and is tender to the bite (check packet directions for exact times).

3.   Remove from the heat and leave to stand for 5 minutes.

4.   Just before serving, remove the cinnamon stick. Fluff with a fork to separate the grains and gently stir in the coriander.

MICROWAVE METHOD (See page 215.)

1.   Put the rice, stock, coriander, cumin and mustard seeds and cinnamon into a casserole.

2.   Cook, uncovered, on HIGH for 10 minutes or until the rice is just tender (it may not have absorbed all the stock).

3.   Cover and leave to stand for 5 minutes. Finish as above.

RICE AND BLACK-EYE BEANS

It is well worth making this richly flavoured combination of rice and black beans in this quantity as it will freeze and reheat very successfully. Alternatively, cover uneaten portions and refrigerate for up to two days. Thaw frozen portions before reheating and make sure all reheated food is piping hot throughout before serving.

Serves 4

Approximately 3.5g of fat per serving

1 large aubergine
1 medium onion
1 garlic clove
600ml/1 pint vegetable stock
175g/6 oz long grain white rice
400g can black-eye beans
oil spray
200g can chopped tomatoes
finely grated rind and juice of 1 lemon
2 tbsp clear honey
4 tbsp finely chopped fresh thyme leaves
8 tbsp natural low fat yogurt

1. Cut off the stem of the aubergine and cut the flesh into bite-sized cubes. Peel and thinly slice the onion. Peel and crush the garlic.

2. Bring the stock to the boil in a saucepan and stir in the rice. Cover tightly and cook over low heat for 12 minutes or until the stock has been absorbed and the rice is tender to the bite. Drain and rinse the beans with cold water.

3. Preheat a non-stick fry-pan and spray with oil. Add the onion and garlic and cook over medium heat, stirring occasionally, until pale golden brown. Add the aubergine, tomatoes, lemon rind and juice and

the honey. Reduce the heat to low, cover the pan and cook for 10-15 minutes, stirring once or twice, or until the aubergine is tender.

4. Add the rice, beans and thyme. Cook for 1-2 minutes until bubbling hot.

5. Season to taste and serve, topped with the yogurt.

MICROWAVE METHOD (See page 215.)

1. *Cut off the stem of the aubergine and cut the flesh into bite-sized cubes. Peel and thinly slice the onion. Peel and crush the garlic.*

2. *Put the rice and HOT stock into a casserole and cook, uncovered, on HIGH for 10 minutes. Cover and leave to stand.*

3. *On the hob, preheat a non-stick fry-pan and spray with oil. Add the onion and garlic and cook over medium heat, stirring occasionally, until pale golden brown. Add the aubergine, tomatoes, lemon rind and juice and the honey. Reduce the heat to low, cover the pan and cook for 10-15 minutes, stirring once or twice, or until the aubergine is tender.*

4. *Add the rice, beans and thyme. Cook for 1-2 minutes until bubbling hot.*

5. *Season to taste and serve, topped with the yogurt.*

RICE WITH GARDEN VEGETABLES

This is really a complete meal but I sometimes serve it with grilled meat, poultry or fish. Or I might stir in a handful of cooked and peeled prawns with the spinach.

It is important to use the young tender leaves of spinach, as they 'cook' just with the heat of the rice. You will find packs of such spinach in supermarkets amongst the salad leaves, with the added bonus of being already washed.

Serves 2

Approximately 12g of fat per serving

175g/6 oz long grain white rice
finely grated rind and juice of 1 lemon
600ml/1 pt vegetable stock
250g/9 oz small courgettes
1 bunch spring onions
1 garlic clove
200g/7 oz pack ready-to-cook young spinach leaves
1 tbsp toasted sesame oil
freshly milled salt and black pepper

1. Cook the rice to packet directions, using the lemon rind, juice and the stock as the liquid.

2. Meanwhile, trim the courgettes and spring onions and cut into slices. Peel and crush the garlic. Roll the spinach leaves (like a cigar) and cut across into thin slices.

3.	Lightly stir the spinach into the hot rice, cover and keep warm.

4.	Heat the oil in a large non-stick fry-pan or wok and add the courgettes, spring onions and garlic. Cook over high heat, stirring constantly, until just soft and golden brown. Season to taste.

5.	Pile the rice and spinach on to warmed plates and spoon the vegetables on top. Serve immediately.

MICROWAVE METHOD (See page 215.)

*1.	Place the rice, lemon rind and juice and HOT stock into a casserole. Cook, uncovered, on HIGH for 10 minutes or until the stock has been absorbed and the rice is tender. Lightly stir the spinach into the rice, cover and keep warm.*

*2.	Meanwhile, trim the courgettes and spring onions and cut into slices. Peel and crush the garlic. Roll the spinach leaves (like a cigar) and cut across into thin slices.*

*3.	On the hob, heat the oil in a large non-stick fry-pan or wok and add the courgettes, spring onions and garlic. Cook over high heat, stirring constantly, until just soft and golden brown. Season to taste. Serve as above.*

POLENTA AND LENTILS

This is another dish that comes under the category, for me, of 'comfort food'. With its bright and cheering pepper mixture and very satisfying soft polenta, this is a good dish to serve on a miserable wet day. Toast some chunky slices of Ciabatta bread and spread with roasted garlic (page 201), Tomato or my low fat Pesto (pages 190 and 192) to serve alongside. If you are very hungry, add a lightly poached egg to each serving.

Always buy peppers that are firm to the feel in the hand, never any that are soft and blotchy as they are past their prime. Red, yellow and orange peppers are green peppers which have been allowed to ripen and consequently are much sweeter in taste. Tip the unused lentils into a non-metallic container (do not leave in the can) and refrigerate. Use within two days as a salad (mix with a little dressing and some chopped spring onions), in a casserole or stir into a soup.

Serves 2

Approximately 4.5g of fat per serving

1 medium red pepper
1 medium yellow or orange pepper
1 medium onion
2 garlic cloves
½ a 400g can green lentils
1 tsp clear honey
2 tbsp balsamic or sherry vinegar
freshly milled salt and black pepper
600ml/1 pint vegetable stock
115g/4 oz instant polenta
1 tbsp sun-dried tomato paste

1. Quarter the peppers and remove the stems, any white pith and the seeds. Place under a hot grill until blackened and blistered. Drop into a plastic bag, seal the open end and leave until cool enough to handle. You will then find it easy to strip off the skins. Cut the flesh into strips.

2. Meanwhile, peel the onion and cut into thin slices. Separate into rings. Peel and crush the garlic. Drain the lentils (see opposite).

3. Put the onion and honey into a non-stick fry-pan, cover and cook over medium heat until golden brown and very soft, stirring once or twice. Add the garlic, peppers, lentils and vinegar. Season to taste, stir to combine, then cover and keep warm.

4. Using a non-stick pan, bring the stock to the boil. Stir in the polenta and cook, stirring constantly, over medium heat for around 5 minutes or until the texture is soft and creamy and the polenta comes away from the sides of the pan. Beat in the tomato paste and season with pepper.

5. If necessary, heat the lentil mixture until bubbling hot.

6. Serve the polenta on to warm plates and spoon the lentil sauce on top.

MICROWAVE METHOD FOR THE SAUCE (See page 215.)

3. *Place the onion and honey in a casserole, cover and cook on HIGH for about 3 minutes or until soft. Add the garlic, peppers, lentils and vinegar. Stir to combine and cook on MEDIUM for 2-3 minutes or until piping hot. Keep warm.*

BUTTERNUT SQUASH AND CHICKPEA CURRY

The slight sweetness of the squash marries well with the nuttiness of the chickpeas in this quickly cooked curry. It provides two very generous portions so only serve with rice if you are very hungry but some bread would be useful to mop up the sauce. Traditionally-made Indian Naan bread, delicious though it may be, is high in fat so look for the new lower-fat variety which weighs in at around 2% fat per bread. Sprinkle with water and pop under a hot grill for about 3 minutes, then serve piping hot.

Different varieties of curry paste vary in fat content, I have taken an average.

Serves 2

Approximately 7.5g of fat per serving

1 medium onion
1 small butternut squash – about 600g/1¼ lb
1 medium carrot
1 garlic clove
400g can chickpeas
115g/5½ oz Swiss chard leaves or spinach
4 tbsp natural yogurt
freshly milled salt and black pepper
1 tbsp curry paste
1 tbsp finely chopped or grated fresh ginger
200g can chopped tomatoes
200ml/7 fl oz vegetable stock

1. Peel and finely chop the onion. Cut the squash into quarters and remove and discard the stem and seeds. Peel the flesh and cut into bite-sized pieces. Peel and dice the carrot. Peel and crush the garlic. Drain the chickpeas. Wash and drain the chard. Season the yogurt with salt and pepper.

2. Put the onion into a non-stick pan (or wok) and cook, stirring, over high heat for a few minutes until it begins to brown. Add the squash, carrot and garlic and cook for 2-3 minutes.

3. Stir in the curry paste, ginger, tomatoes, chickpeas and stock. Bring to the boil, then cover and cook over low heat for about 15 minutes, stirring occasionally, or until the vegetables are tender (so that you can break up the squash with a fork). If the curry gets a little dry while cooking, stir in a spoonful or two of boiling water.

4. Cook the chard in a saucepan with a little water for 3-4 minutes, or until just tender. Drain and roughly chop.

5. Season the curry and spoon on to warmed plates. Pile the chard on top and spoon over the seasoned yogurt.

MICROWAVE METHOD

The chard (or spinach) can be cooked on HIGH for 2 minutes.

BULGAR WHEAT SALAD

This is another 'dip-into' salad that is so useful during the warmer months when spending long hours in the kitchen has lost its appeal. Like all grain, rice and pasta salads, the flavours come through best if the salad is eaten at room temperature rather than straight from the refrigerator. It is delicious and satisfying simply served with some fresh salad vegetables such as sliced tomatoes or crisp lettuce leaves. The salad also goes very well with Spiced Chicken (page 158) or any grilled or barbecued meats.

Bulgar wheat (may also be spelt burghul or bulgur) consists of wheat kernels which have been steamed, dried then crushed, making it very quick to prepare. Toasted sesame oil has a richer flavour than the lighter variety but either will be fine.

This recipe makes four servings but will keep in the refrigerator for up to 48 hours.

Serves 4

Approximately 9.5g of fat per serving

115g/4 oz ready-to-eat dried apricots
50ml/2 fl oz orange juice
300ml/½ pint vegetable stock
225g/8 oz bulgar wheat
1 tbsp toasted sesame oil
6 spring onions
2 oranges
finely grated rind and juice of 1 large lemon
freshly milled salt and black pepper

1.   At least one hour before cooking: Cut the apricots into fine slivers (easiest with scissors). Put them in a bowl with the orange juice and leave to soak for at least 1 hour.

2.   Put the stock into a saucepan and bring to the boil. Remove the pan from the heat, stir in the bulgar wheat and cover. Leave to stand for about 5 minutes or until the grains have absorbed all the liquid.

3.   Tip the wheat into a large serving bowl, drizzle the oil over the top and gently mix through with a fork. Cover with a tea-towel and leave to cool at room temperature.

4.   Meanwhile, trim the spring onions and cut into thin slices. Using a sharp knife, cut away all the white peel and pith from the oranges. Holding the fruit over a bowl to catch the juice, cut between each orange segment allowing it to drop into the bowl.

5.   Add the apricots and any remaining juice, the spring onions, orange segments and the juice in the bowl, the lemon rind and juice to the bulgar wheat. Gently fold together keeping the orange segments whole. Season to taste before serving.

SMOKED TROUT KEDGEREE

Kedgeree, originally a simple Indian spiced rice dish, was embellished in the 18th century by English cooks who added smoked fish, hard-boiled eggs and a rich, creamy sauce, making the dish which, then, was part of a hearty English breakfast. Tastes have changed and versions of the dish would now be more likely eaten at lunch or supper. Still with the same basic ingredients, this recipe is full of flavour but much lighter than its namesake.

You will find bottles of mint jelly (not to be confused with mint sauce) in the sauce section of supermarkets. Made to serve with lamb, it adds a sweet tangy flavour to the cucumber sauce which would go well with any curry dish.

Serves 2

Approximately 11g of fat per serving

1 medium onion
1 garlic clove
oil spray
175g/6 oz long grain white rice
1 tsp curry paste
600ml/1 pint hot vegetable stock
¼ of a cucumber
2 tbsp mint jelly
150ml/5 fl oz natural yogurt
Freshly milled salt and black pepper
175g/6 oz smoked trout fillets
1 tbsp very finely chopped fresh coriander

To serve:
lemon wedges

1.	Peel the onion and cut into thin slices. Peel and crush the garlic.

2.   Lightly spray a non-stick pan with oil and add the onion. Cook, covered, over a low heat until very soft, stirring once or twice.

3.   Stir in the garlic, rice and curry paste. Add the stock, stir, then cover and cook over medium heat for 10-15 minutes, stirring occasionally, until the rice is tender and has absorbed the stock.

4.   Meanwhile, cut the cucumber into quarters lengthways and scoop out the seeds (easiest with a serrated-edged spoon). Cut the flesh into small cubes. Put the mint jelly and yogurt into a bowl and whisk until smooth. Add seasoning to taste, then stir in the cucumber.

5.   Break the trout into bite-sized pieces.

6.   Fork the coriander into the hot rice.

7.   Pile the rice on to warmed plates, arrange the trout on the top and spoon the cucumber sauce on one side. Garnish with the lemon wedges and serve.

MICROWAVE METHOD (See page 215.)

1.   As opposite.

2.   Put the onion into a casserole and lightly spray with oil. Cook, covered, on HIGH for 2-3 minutes or until very soft.

3.   Stir in the garlic, rice and curry paste. Add the HOT stock and cook, uncovered, on HIGH for 10 minutes. Cover and leave to stand for 5 minutes.

4.   Complete the recipe as above.

COUSCOUS STUFFED PEPPERS

Serve with lots of good bread to mop up the dressing and a platter of chilled fruits such as the Balsamic Strawberries (page 211). Refrigerate any uneaten portions and serve at room temperature the next day.

Serves 4   *Approximately 8g of fat per serving*

4 yellow peppers
225ml/8 fl oz vegetable stock
75g/3 oz couscous
2 ripe tomatoes
1 large onion
2 tbsp olive oil
2 tsp clear honey
3 large lemons
50g/2 oz raisins
2 tbsp finely chopped fresh mint
2 tbsp finely chopped fresh coriander
freshly milled salt and black pepper

1. Slice the tops off the peppers, keeping the stems intact, and set aside. Scoop out the seeds and any white pith inside the peppers. Pack the peppers in a deep casserole (or a soufflé dish) just large enough to hold them upright.

2. Bring the stock to the boil in a large pan, add the couscous, stir to combine, cover and leave to stand for 5 minutes. Cover the tomatoes with boiling water. Leave to stand for 5 minutes. Drain, cut out the stem end and slip off the skins. Cut each tomato in half and scoop out the seeds. Roughly chop the flesh and add to the couscous. Peel and finely chop the onion.

3. Heat 1 tbsp of the oil in a non-stick fry-pan, add the onion and drizzle the honey over the top. Cook over a low heat, stirring occasionally, for

about 10 minutes or until very soft and golden brown. Remove from the heat. Finely grate the rind and squeeze the juice of one of the lemons and add to the onion.

4. Add the onion, the raisins and half the mint and coriander to the couscous and tomatoes. Gently stir together and season to taste.

5. Heat the oven to 180°C/gas mark 4. Spoon the stuffing into the peppers, gently pressing it in with the back of a small spoon. Replace the reserved tops. Add 4 tbsp water to the dish; cover with a lid or foil. Place in the hot oven and cook for about 45 minutes or until the peppers are soft when pierced with a fork. Remove from the oven but leave covered. Allow to cool until quite cold (or refrigerate overnight).

6. Lift the peppers on to a serving platter. Put the remaining oil and herbs, the juice of the two remaining lemons and the juices in the baking dish into a small bowl. Whisk to combine, season to taste and spoon over the peppers. Leave to marinate for an hour before serving.

MICROWAVE METHOD (See page 215.)

1–4. As above.

5. Fill the peppers as above and add the water to the casserole. Cover and cook on MEDIUM-HIGH for about 30 minutes or until the peppers are soft when pierced with a fork. Complete the recipe as above.

LENTIL AND CHICKEN SALAD

Quick and easy, a great dish to make when you get home from work. The tamarind paste in the dressing adds a rich sweet-sour flavour which goes well with the smoky taste of the lentils, while the watercress or rocket is a peppery contrast.

Serves 2

11g fat per serving

1 skinned and boned chicken breast – about 175g/6 oz
1 tsp soft brown sugar
1 tsp paprika
pinch of chilli powder
freshly milled salt and black pepper
1 large onion
1 garlic clove
400g can green lentils
225g/8 oz ripe tomatoes
1 tbsp olive oil
2 tbsp white wine vinegar
2 tbsp tamarind paste
watercress or rocket leaves

1. Cut the chicken diagonally into thin slices. Spoon the sugar, paprika and chilli powder into a plastic food bag, add a good seasoning of pepper and the chicken. Twist the end to close and shake to coat the chicken evenly with the spices.

2. Peel the onion, cut into thin slices and separate into rings. Peel and crush the garlic. Tip the lentils into a strainer and leave to drain. Thinly slice the tomatoes and arrange on two plates.

3. Heat a non-stick wok and add the chicken. Cook over high heat for 3-4 minutes, stirring constantly, until golden brown and cooked through. Remove from the pan and keep warm.

4. Add the onion to the pan (no need to wash it first) and cook over medium high heat, stirring occasionally, until soft and brown. Stir in the garlic, oil, vinegar, tamarind paste and the drained lentils.

5. Bring just to the boil, then remove from the heat. Stir in the chicken and season to taste.

6. Pile on top of the tomato slices, add some sprigs of watercress or rocket leaves and serve immediately.

TOMATO POLENTA WITH BEAN RAGOUT

Traditional polenta takes nearly an hour to cook, constantly stirred, but the quick-cook variety is easy to find in most shops and is ready in just 2-3 minutes. Topped with a sauce made with a can of beans, this dish is fast food with a difference. Serve with some crusty bread to mop up the sauce.

Purchased pesto sauce contains over 5g of fat per tablespoon but, if you make the recipe on page 192, it has only 4g per tablespoon.

Serves 2

Approximately 6g of fat per serving

3 sun-dried tomatoes (dry-packed)
350ml/12 fl oz vegetable stock
125g/4½ oz quick-cook polenta
400g can cannellini beans
8 cherry tomatoes
1 medium-sized onion
1 garlic clove
oil spray
1 tbsp pesto sauce
freshly milled salt and black pepper

1.   Cut the dried tomatoes into thin slivers and put into a bowl. Cover with boiling water and leave for 5 minutes, then drain.

2. Pour the stock into a pan and bring to the boil. Sprinkle in the polenta and cook, stirring constantly, for 2-3 minutes or until thick and smooth. Stir in the soaked tomatoes. Spoon on to a non-stick baking sheet and spread into a square about 2.5cm/1 in thick. Leave to cool slightly.

3. Drain the beans. Halve the cherry tomatoes. Peel and thinly slice the onion. Peel and crush the garlic.

4. Preheat a griddle or non-stick fry-pan. Cut the polenta into four portions and lightly spray with oil on both sides. Cook on the hot griddle or fry-pan until golden brown on both sides.

5. Meanwhile, put the onion into a non-stick pan and cook over medium heat, stirring, until soft and brown. Stir in the garlic, beans, tomatoes and pesto sauce. Season to taste and gently heat until piping hot.

6. Arrange two pieces of polenta on each warmed plate and spoon the beans on top

POLENTA WITH CHILLI TOMATOES

In this quickly made dish the richly flavoured tomatoes both look and taste delicious paired with smooth golden yellow polenta.

I pile the polenta into warm shallow bowls, spoon the sauce on top and serve it with grilled Ciabatta bread.

For a touch of garlic, rub the bread with a peeled garlic clove before toasting or, if you have some roasted garlic handy (see page 201), spread on the hot toast.

If you are really hungry, increase the amount of polenta to 175g/6 oz and the stock to 900ml/1½ pints (this will make the fat count approximately 8g of fat per serving).

Serves 2

Approximately 7g of fat per serving

225g/8 oz ripe tomatoes, the plum variety if available
2 tsp oil
1-2 tbsp sweet chilli sauce (to taste)
2 tsp clear honey
600ml/1 pint vegetable stock
115g/4 oz instant polenta
freshly milled salt and black pepper

1. Cut the tomatoes in half through the stem (and into quarters if large) and place in a bowl. Whisk together the oil, chilli sauce and honey. Pour over the tomatoes and gently stir to coat them evenly.

2. Line a grill pan with foil (to make washing-up easier) and add the tomatoes, spreading them in a single layer. Drizzle over any chilli mixture remaining in the bowl.

3. Place under a hot grill and cook until soft and golden brown, stirring and turning over once or twice (try not to break up the tomatoes as you do this, they look prettier if they remain whole).

4. Meanwhile, bring the stock to the boil in a non-stick pan. Stir in the polenta and cook, stirring constantly, over medium heat for around 5 minutes or until the texture is soft and creamy and the polenta comes away from the sides of the pan. Beat in seasoning to taste.

5. Pile the polenta into warm shallow bowls and spoon the tomatoes and their juices on top. Serve piping hot.

POLENTA WITH MUSHROOM AND RATATOUILLE SAUCE

This sauce goes just as well with rice or pasta. If you have some homemade Pesto or Tomato Pesto (pages 190–192) in the fridge, omit the sage and stir a little pesto into the polenta after cooking. Remember to add the extra grams of fat if you are seriously counting. With a green salad you have a quick substantial meal.

Serves 2   *Approximately 7g of fat per serving*

4-5 fresh sage leaves
115g/4 oz button mushrooms
400g can ratatouille
1 tbsp red wine or sherry vinegar
freshly milled salt and black pepper
600ml/1 pint chicken or vegetable stock
115g/4 oz quick cooking polenta

1. Cut the sage leaves into thin shreds. Trim the mushrooms, cutting in half if large.

2. Heat a non-stick fry-pan and add the mushrooms. Cook over medium heat, stirring occasionally, until just golden brown. Add the ratatouille and vinegar and bring just to the boil. Remove from the heat and season to taste. Cover and keep warm.

3. Using a non-stick pan, bring the stock to the boil, then gradually stir in the polenta. Cook, stirring constantly, over medium heat for around 5 minutes or until the texture is soft and creamy and the polenta comes away from the sides of the pan.

4. Gently stir in the sage (or pesto).

5. Pile the polenta on to warmed plates and spoon the hot sauce on top. Serve immediately.

BLACK BEAN HUMMUS

A bowl of this chunky version of hummus (kept covered in the fridge for up to four days) is handy for a quick meal served with wedges of Cos or Little Gem lettuce, sliced tomatoes and crusty bread. Or it can be spooned into a split pitta bread or soft bap and topped with shredded lettuce for a picnic or desk lunch.

If you haven't any tahini spread (made of ground sesame seeds), use 2 tbsp peanut butter, either smooth or chunky. It changes the flavour slightly but the spread is still as delicious. A lemon tastes sharper than a lime, but you can use one here if you haven't got a lime. If you prefer a mellow garlic flavour, use Roasted Garlic (page 201).

Serves 4   *Approximately 7g of fat per serving*

400g can chickpeas
2 cloves garlic
finely grated rind and juice of 1 lime
2 tbsp tahini paste or peanut butter
400g can black eye beans
freshly milled salt and black pepper

1. Tip the chickpeas into a strainer to drain. Peel and chop the garlic.

2. Place the chickpeas, garlic, rind and juice of the lime and the tahini paste (or peanut butter) into a processor. Buzz until smooth.

3. Tip the black beans into the strainer and shake to remove all the liquid.

4. Add to the processor. Buzz just until roughly chopped. Don't process too long as you want a chunky texture.

5. Spoon the spread into a bowl and season to taste.

4
VEGETABLES

ROASTED ONIONS

Onions are often overlooked as a main vegetable and are relegated to being just an indispensable flavouring ingredient. This recipe turns them a rich golden brown with a melting texture which goes well with simply grilled meat or poultry. As part of a non-meat meal, serve the onions with creamy mashed potatoes and a crisply cooked green vegetable and no-one will miss the meat.

Onions grown in warmer areas tend to be sweeter than those grown in northern climates. Look for mild sweet onions such as Spanish or the American Vidalias. The amount of fat in curry pastes varies from 5-8g per tablespoon so I have taken an average count.

Serves 2   *Approximately 8.5g of fat per serving*

2 large sweet onions, about 225g/8 oz each
50ml/2 fl oz clear honey
2 tsp oil
1 tsp paprika
1 tbsp mild curry paste
freshly milled salt and black pepper

1. Preheat the oven to 180°C/gas mark 4. Peel the onions and cut in half crossways.

2. Place the onions, cut sides down, in a baking dish and sprinkle with 1 tbsp cold water. Cover with foil and bake for 30 minutes.

3. Combine the honey, oil, paprika and curry paste.

4. Remove the foil and turn the onions cut side up. Spoon the honey mixture over the top and add a good seasoning of salt and pepper. Return to the oven for about another 30 minutes or until tender, basting with the pan juices once or twice. Serve piping hot.

AUBERGINE AU GRATIN

In the traditional Italian dish called Eggplant Parmegian, the slices of aubergine are fried before layering with the sauce. Grilling is a much better and easier method, reducing the fat content without losing any of the flavour. The addition of a chilli to the recipe adds extra bite to the sauce but is optional. If preferred, a teaspoon or so of sweet chilli sauce would add a softer warm depth to the flavour.

A crisp tossed salad of mixed leaves dressed with a lemony dressing would be a suitable accompaniment.

Serves 2

Approximately 6g of fat per serving

1 small onion
1 garlic clove
1 fresh green chilli
200g can chopped tomatoes
1 tbsp tomato purée
1 tbsp fresh thyme leaves
freshly milled salt and black pepper
1 aubergine – about 450g/1 lb
50g/2 oz fresh breadcrumbs
25g/1 oz finely grated mature Cheddar cheese

1. Peel the onion and finely chop. Peel and crush the garlic. Halve the chilli, discarding the stem and seeds. Thinly slice the flesh. (Wash your hands after preparing chillies as they can irritate the skin.)

2. Put the onion into a non-stick saucepan and cook over medium heat, stirring, for 2-3 minutes or until the onion starts to brown. Add the garlic, chilli, tomatoes, tomato purée and thyme. Cover and cook over low heat for 5 minutes. Season to taste.

3.   Cut off the stem of the aubergine and cut the flesh crosswise into 1.25cm/1 in slices. Arrange in a single layer on a non-stick baking sheet and slip under a preheated grill. Cook for about 5 minutes, turning once, until golden brown. (Or cook on a hot griddle pan until golden brown.)

4.   Preheat the oven to 180°C/gas mark 4. Arrange layers of aubergine and sauce in a shallow oven-proof dish. Combine the breadcrumbs and cheese and spoon evenly over the top.

5.   Place in the hot oven and bake for 25-30 minutes or until bubbling hot and golden brown. For easier cutting and serving leave to stand for 5 minutes.

MICROWAVE METHOD FOR THE SAUCE (See page 215.)

2.   *Put the onion into a casserole, cover and cook on HIGH for 1-2 minutes or until soft. Add the garlic, chilli, tomatoes, tomato purée and thyme. Cover and cook on HIGH for 5 minutes, stirring once. Complete the recipe as above.*

MICROWAVE + GRILL METHOD

2.   *Make the sauce using microwave mode only.*

3.   *Prepare the aubergine and cook under the grill as above.*

4.   *Assemble the dish as above.*

5.   *Stand the dish on a low rack and cook on MEDIUM + GRILL for 10-15 minutes or until the vegetables are bubbling hot and the top golden brown.*

AUBERGINE SALAD AND CHICKEN WRAPS

This recipe is based on a North African dish and is an unusual way to cook aubergine. I have suggested serving it with grilled chicken and the fashionable bread 'wraps' now in our stores but it is also excellent served as a salad dish, especially with the Couscous Salad with Mint and Tomatoes on page 182. The chicken, which has a delicious orange and mustard glaze, could be cooked on a barbecue.

The salad is best made several hours before serving to allow the flavours to mellow. The recipe serves four and will keep in the refrigerator for 24 hours.

Serves 4

Approximately 6g of fat per serving (excluding the wraps)

1 large aubergine – about 450g/1 lb
3 garlic cloves
freshly milled salt and black pepper
375g/12 oz ripe plum tomatoes
2 tsp olive oil
2 tbsp red wine vinegar
2 tsp harissa paste (or more if wished)
a good handful of chopped fresh mint
1 tbsp soy sauce
1 tbsp finely cut orange marmalade
2 tsp wholegrain mustard
2 skinned and boned chicken breasts, about
  140g/5 oz each
1 packet of 'wraps'

1. At least 2 hours before serving: Trim and peel the aubergine, cut into cubes and put into a saucepan. Peel the garlic and add to the pan with sufficient water to cover the aubergine. Add a good pinch of salt, then cover and cook over medium heat for about 15 minutes, stirring once or twice, or until soft.

2. Tip the aubergine and garlic into a colander to drain, then, still in the colander, press with a fork to remove all the water.

3. Meanwhile, cover the tomatoes with boiling water and leave to stand for a few minutes. Drain, slip off the skins and cut into thin slices, discarding the stem ends. Place in a non-stick pan and cook over a low heat, stirring occasionally, for about 15 minutes or until they have reduced to a sauce.

4. Stir in the oil, vinegar, harissa paste, mint and the aubergine. Stir thoroughly and season to taste. Spoon into a bowl, cool, cover and refrigerate for at least 2-3 hours.

5. To serve: combine the soy sauce, marmalade and mustard in a shallow dish and add the chicken, turning to coat it with the glaze on all sides.

6. Preheat a non-stick fry-pan, griddle, grill or the barbecue. Cook the chicken for about 5-6 minutes on each side, turning once, or until tender and a rich golden brown.

7. Cut the chicken diagonally into thin slices. Place on a wrap with a spoonful of Aubergine Salad, roll up and eat.

CAULIFLOWER AND LENTIL CURRY

I like to serve this curry with a selection of traditional 'sambals' such as a sliced banana or apple wedges, mango chutney, sultanas, lemon wedges or thinly sliced cucumber, all served in small bowls for each person to help themselves. They are very quick to assemble while the curry is cooking and make a simple dish into a feast. If I am really hungry I serve the curry with Basmati rice or just some good bread.

Make sure you use red lentils; they don't need soaking before cooking.

Serves 2   *Approximately 4.5g of fat per serving*

115g/4 oz red lentils
1 medium onion
1 garlic clove
1 small cauliflower or about 225g/8 oz florets
1 tsp oil
½ tsp ground turmeric
½ tsp ground coriander
½ tsp ground cumin
finely grated rind and juice of 1 lemon
2 tsp chilli sauce
450ml/¾ pint vegetable stock
2 tbsp mint jelly
150ml/5 fl oz natural low fat yogurt
freshly milled salt and black pepper
3 tbsp finely chopped fresh coriander

1. Place the lentils in a sieve and rinse under cold water, then leave to drain. Peel and finely chop the onion, peel and crush the garlic. Prepare the cauliflower and break the florets into bite-sized pieces.

2. Put the oil, onion and garlic into a non-stick saucepan and cook over low heat, stirring occasionally, until very soft and just starting to brown.

3.   Stir in the turmeric, ground coriander and cumin and cook, stirring, for 1 minute. Add the lentils, lemon rind and juice, chilli sauce and stock.

4.   Bring just to the boil, stir well, then cover and cook over a low heat for about 20 minutes, stirring occasionally, until very soft.

5.   Meanwhile, whisk the mint jelly into the yogurt, spoon into a small bowl and chill until required.

6.   When the lentils are almost soft, cook the cauliflower in lightly salted water for about 5 minutes until just tender (do not overcook). Drain.

7.   Beat the lentil sauce with a wooden spoon until almost smooth and season to taste. Stir in the cauliflower and place over a low heat for 1-2 minutes or until piping hot.

8.   Serve the curry sprinkled with the fresh coriander, the minted yogurt and the sambals (to be added as required).

MICROWAVE METHOD (See page 215.)

1.   As opposite.

2.   Put the oil, onion and garlic into a casserole, cover and cook on HIGH for 1-2 minutes or until soft.

3.   Stir in the turmeric, ground coriander, cumin, lentils, lemon rind and juice, chilli sauce and HOT stock.

4.   Cover (with a vented lid) and cook on HIGH for 12-15 minutes, stirring once, or until the lentils are very soft.

5.   Complete the recipe as above.

COURGETTES AND PEPPERS WITH ORANGE

I make this in bulk when the vegetables are in season and inexpensive, spoon it into suitable containers and freeze it away for the winter.

Serve it piping hot with meat or fish, warm or cold as part of a salad plate or stirred into cooked rice or pasta to make a more substantial salad dish. For a quick snack, cut a big soft roll or a pitta bread almost through, open out and fill with the vegetables. Gently squash to flatten slightly, then enjoy.

Serves 4   *Approximately 1.5g of fat per serving*

1 large onion
1 red pepper
1 yellow or orange pepper
4 small courgettes
1 large orange
2 garlic cloves
150ml/¼ pint vegetable stock
1 tbsp clear honey
several sprigs of fresh thyme
freshly milled salt and black pepper

1. Peel the onion and cut in half through the stem and root ends. Cut each half in thin slices to give you half-moons. Cut the peppers in half, removing and discarding the stems, seeds and any white pith. Cut the flesh into thick slices. Trim and slice the courgettes. Remove the zest of the orange using the fine side of a cheese grater, then extract the juice. Peel and crush the garlic.

2. Put the onion into a large non-stick pan (I use a wok), cover and cook over medium heat for about 5 minutes, stirring once or twice, or until soft and just beginning to brown.

3.   Add the peppers, courgettes, orange rind and juice, the garlic, stock, honey and thyme.

4.   Over high heat, bring just to the boil. Stir well, then cover and cook over a low heat for about 20 minutes, stirring occasionally, or until the vegetables are just cooked.

5.   If there is a lot of liquid, increase the heat and cook uncovered for a few minutes. There should be just a few spoonfuls of liquid remaining in the pan.

6.   Season to taste, then serve immediately or when required.

MICROWAVE METHOD (See page 215.)

1.   As opposite.

2.   Put the onion into a large casserole, cover and cook on HIGH for about 3 minutes or until soft.

3.   Add the peppers, courgettes, orange rind and juice, the garlic, stock, honey and thyme.

4.   Bring just to the boil on HIGH for about 3 minutes. Stir well, then cover and cook on HIGH for about 10-12 minutes, stirring occasionally, or until the vegetables are just cooked.

5.   If there is a lot of liquid, cook, uncovered, on HIGH for a minute or two. There should be just a few spoonfuls of liquid remaining in the casserole.

6.   Season to taste and serve immediately or when required.

GREEN BEANS WITH TOMATOES

A simple way to make green beans more interesting.
Serve hot or at room temperature.

Serves 2

Approximately 3g of fat per serving

225g/8 oz runner or thin green beans
2 garlic cloves
1 tsp olive oil
1 tsp fennel seeds
½ tsp chilli sauce
230g can chopped tomatoes
1 tbsp red wine vinegar
freshly milled salt and black pepper

1. Trim the runner beans and, holding the knife at an
    angle, cut into thin slices. Or trim the green beans
    and cut into short lengths. Peel and crush the
    garlic.

2. Heat the oil in a non-stick pan, add the garlic and
    cook briefly over medium heat (do not allow to
    burn) just to soften. Stir in the fennel seeds, then
    the chilli sauce, tomatoes and vinegar.

3. Bring just to the boil, add the beans and stir to combine.

4. Cover and cook over low heat, stirring frequently, for about 10 minutes or until the beans are tender and the sauce slightly thickened.

5. Season to taste.

MICROWAVE METHOD (See page 215.)

1. *Trim the runner beans and, holding the knife at an angle, cut into thin slices. Or trim the green beans and cut into short lengths. Peel and crush the garlic.*

2. *Put the oil and garlic into a casserole, cover and cook on HIGH for 1 minute. Stir in the fennel seeds, then the chilli sauce, tomatoes and vinegar.*

3. *Cover and cook on HIGH for 2 minutes to bring just to the boil.*

4. *Stir in the beans, cover and cook on MEDIUM-HIGH for about 6 minutes or until the beans are tender. Season to taste.*

MARINATED MUSHROOMS WITH TOMATO AND THYME

Mushrooms absorb flavour yet keep their texture and shape even after several hours of refrigeration. Just stir lightly before serving and enjoy as part of a salad plate with cold meats or Herbed Yogurt Cheese (page 189). When really busy, I spoon some of the mushrooms into a soft bap, give it a gentle squash and eat it on the run!

Boiling the cooking juices concentrates the flavours and produces a rich dressing for the mushrooms; marinating overnight allows them to absorb the spicy flavours. They keep in the fridge for up to 48 hours. The tiny baby button mushrooms look most attractive when cooked, but if you buy the larger button mushrooms, cut each into three or four thick slices before cooking.

Serves 4

Approximately 4g of fat per serving

375g/12 oz baby button mushrooms
1 large onion
3 garlic cloves
6 dry-pack sun-dried tomatoes
1 tbsp olive oil
1 tsp ground cumin
1 tbsp fennel seeds
1 tbsp tomato purée
75ml/2½ fl oz vegetable stock
2 tbsp red wine vinegar
2 tbsp dry white vermouth
2 tbsp fresh thyme leaves
freshly milled salt and black pepper

To serve: finely chopped fresh parsley

1. Trim the stems of the mushrooms and wipe with a tea-towel if needed. Peel and very thinly slice the

onion, then separate into rings. Peel and crush the garlic. Cut the sun-dried tomatoes into slivers (easiest with scissors).

2.   Put the oil and onion into a large non-stick pan (I use a wok), cover and cook over low heat, stirring occasionally, until soft.

3.   Add the garlic, cumin, fennel seeds, mushrooms, sun-dried tomatoes, tomato purée, stock, vinegar, vermouth and thyme. Cover and cook over low heat for 10 minutes, stirring once or twice.

4.   Using a perforated spoon, place the mushrooms in a serving bowl. Bring the juices in the pan to the boil and boil for about 3-4 minutes or until they have reduced and are syrupy. Cool slightly, then pour over the mushrooms. Leave to cool, then cover and refrigerate overnight.

5.   Before serving, check whether they need any more seasoning. Serve sprinkled with freshly chopped parsley.

MICROWAVE METHOD (See page 215.)

1.   Prepare the ingredients as above.

2.   Put the oil and onion into a casserole, cover and cook for 3 minutes on HIGH or until soft. Stir in the garlic, cumin, fennel seeds, mushrooms, sun-dried tomatoes, tomato purée, stock, vinegar, vermouth and thyme. Cover and cook on MEDIUM-HIGH for 8 minutes.

4.   Using a perforated spoon, place the mushrooms in a serving bowl. Cook the juices in the casserole, uncovered, on HIGH for about 3 minutes or until they have reduced and are syrupy. Cool slightly, then pour over the mushrooms. Continue as above.

PEPPERS WITH MUSHROOMS AND COURGETTES

As a change from the more usual rice or grains, these peppers are filled with a mixture of mushrooms, courgettes and aubergines, plus a touch of sweetness provided by the sultanas. In the winter I serve them freshly cooked with a baked jacket potato. In warmer weather, I leave them to cool to room temperature, then serve with some crisp green salad leaves such as Cos or Romaine tossed with Honey and Mustard Dressing (page 177). Why not double up on the ingredients and so make enough for two meals?

Serves 2   *Approximately 3.5g of fat per serving*

1 small onion
1 garlic clove
1 small aubergine, about 150g/5½ oz
115g/4 oz small courgettes
75g/3 oz button mushrooms
1 tsp olive oil
finely grated rind and juice of 1 lemon
1 tbsp dry white wine or vermouth
4 tbsp tomato purée
2 tbsp sultanas
freshly milled salt and black pepper
2 large red or yellow peppers

1. Peel the onion and finely chop. Peel and crush the garlic. Trim the aubergine and cut into small dice. Trim the courgettes, cut into quarters lengthways and then into slices. Trim the mushrooms and slice thinly.

2. Heat the oil in a large non-stick fry-pan and add the onion. Cook over a low heat for a few minutes or until very soft and beginning to brown. Stir in the garlic, aubergine, courgettes, mushrooms, lemon rind and juice, the vermouth, tomato purée and sultanas.

3. Cover and cook over medium heat for about 15 minutes, stirring once or twice, or until the vegetables are very soft (if the mixture starts to stick to the pan, stir in a dash of hot water). Season to taste.

4. Meanwhile, preheat the oven to 180°C/gas mark 4. Slice the tops off the peppers, keeping the stems intact, and set aside. Scoop out the seeds and any pith inside the peppers. Pack the peppers into a deep casserole (or soufflé dish) just large enough to hold them upright.

5. Fill the peppers with the vegetable mixture, pushing it in gently with the back of a small spoon. Replace the reserved tops. Add 4 tbsp water to the dish, then cover with a lid or foil. Place in the hot oven and cook for about 30 minutes or until the peppers are very soft when pierced with a fork.

6. Serve freshly cooked or leave to cool to room temperature.

MICROWAVE METHOD (See page 215.)

1. *Prepare the vegetables as opposite and in 4 above, putting the peppers into a suitable casserole.*

2. *Put the oil and onion into a large casserole, cover and cook on HIGH for 1 minute. Stir in the other ingredients as above, cover and cook on HIGH for about 15 minutes, stirring once or twice, or until the vegetables are very soft. Season.*

3. *Fill the peppers as above and add 2.5cm/1 in of boiling water to the dish.*

4. *Cover and cook on MEDIUM-HIGH for about 20 minutes or until the peppers are very soft when pierced with a fork.*

POTATO SALADS

When British new potatoes come into season I serve them with just about everything. They only need a quick scrub and to be popped into lightly salted boiling water for just a few minutes until they are fork tender. Sprinkle with crushed sea salt and you won't miss that big knob of butter. If you must, then gently toss them with a teaspoon or so of extra virgin olive oil. They are also superb served at room temperature as a freshly made salad, not dressed with mayonnaise but with crunchy salad onions, a spicy herb paste or any of the dressings on pages 177–178.

Enjoy a plate of poached salmon with one of these potato salads and some crisp wedges of baby lettuce such as Tom Thumb.

Harissa is a warmly-spiced paste made of chillies, garlic and cumin. Initially, use with care until you are sure how highly spiced you want the dish to be. It can be used in any recipe needing chilli flavouring.

SPICED POTATO SALAD

Serves 2　　　　　*Approximately 9g of fat per serving*

375g/12 oz small new potatoes
1-2 tsp harissa paste
1 tbsp olive oil
1 tbsp red wine vinegar
freshly milled salt and black pepper
a good handful of finely chopped fresh mint leaves

1.　Lightly scrub the potatoes and drop into a pan of lightly salted water. Bring to the boil, reduce the heat to low and cook for about 10 minutes or until tender when pierced with a fork. The time depends on the size of the potatoes.

2.　Meanwhile, measure the harissa paste, oil and vinegar into a salad bowl and stir to combine.

3. Drain the potatoes well, then tip into the bowl. Gently stir to coat them with the dressing without breaking them up. Add seasoning to taste and finally, the mint. Serve at room temperature.

MICROWAVE METHOD (See page 215.)

Put the potatoes into a casserole with 4 tbsp water. Cover and cook on MEDIUM-HIGH for about 8 minutes, stirring once, or until just tender when pierced with a fork. Leave for 2-3 minutes, then drain and use as above.

CRUNCHY POTATO SALAD

Serves 2

Approximately 7.5g of fat per serving

375g/12 oz small new potatoes
1 small red onion
4 spring onions
2 tbsp balsamic vinegar
1 tbsp olive oil
freshly milled salt and black pepper

1. *Cook the potatoes as opposite.*

2. *Peel and finely chop the red onion. Trim the spring onions and cut in thin slices.*

3. *Drain the potatoes well and tip into a salad bowl. Immediately spoon over the vinegar and oil and gently stir together. Stir in the red and spring onions and season to taste. Serve at room temperature.*

MICROWAVE METHOD

Follow the microwave method for Spiced Potato Salad above.

RED CABBAGE WITH PEARS

A world away from pickled red cabbage, here this much under-used winter vegetable is cooked to a melting consistency with the added punch of ginger and unexpected fresh pear. Allow time for it to cook slowly or make ahead and reheat. I often double up on the ingredients and freeze half for another day.

As a non-meat meal, I serve the cabbage with a crunchy skinned baked potato and a spoonful of soured cream or low fat créme fraiche. As a side dish, it is perfect with a game casserole, a grilled steak or slices of cold gammon.

Serves 2

Negligible fat per serving

375g/12 oz red cabbage
1 large onion
1-2 garlic cloves
1 tsp ground coriander
2 tbsp clear honey
75ml/3 fl oz apple juice or vegetable stock
1 large just-ripe pear
1 small knob of preserved ginger
1 tbsp sherry vinegar or red wine vinegar
freshly milled salt and black pepper

1. Trim the cabbage, cutting out the centre and any thick stems. Using a large, sharp knife, very finely slice the cabbage into thin shreds, discarding any thick ribs as you cut. Peel the onion and cut into thin slices. Peel and crush the garlic.

2. Put the onion into a large non-stick pan (I use a wok), cover and cook over medium heat, stirring once or twice, until soft and beginning to brown. Stir in the garlic, coriander and honey. Add the cabbage and apple juice (or stock) and stir well.

3. Cover and cook over low heat, stirring occasionally, for about 20 minutes or until the cabbage is very soft.

4. Meanwhile, cut the pear into quarters, removing the peel and core. Cut into chunks. Finely chop the preserved ginger.

5. When the cabbage is very soft, stir in the chunks of pear, the ginger and the vinegar.

6. Continue to cook, stirring gently, just until the pear is tender and the liquid has almost evaporated. Season to taste.

TOMATO GRATIN

Make this simple dish in the summer when locally grown tomatoes are very ripe and bursting with flavour. It goes well with cold ham, both grilled and cold chicken or, my favourite, ready-to-eat smoked trout fillets.

If I have time I skin the tomatoes but it is just as good if you leave them on. A bag of fresh breadcrumbs is a useful item to have in the freezer; you can use them by the handful, still frozen.

Serves 2

Approximately 6g of fat per serving

450g/1 lb ripe tomatoes
oil spray
freshly milled salt and black pepper
1 tbsp sherry vinegar
1 garlic clove
55g/2 oz fresh breadcrumbs
1 tbsp fresh thyme leaves or dried Herbes de Provence
2 tsp sesame or olive oil

1. Preheat the oven to 180°C/gas mark 4.

2. Put the tomatoes into a bowl and cover with boiling water. Leave to stand for 5 minutes, then drain, cut out the stem ends and slip off the skins. Lightly spray a shallow baking dish with oil.

3. Cut the tomatoes into thick slices and arrange, slightly overlapping, in the baking dish. Sprinkle with salt and pepper and drizzle the vinegar over the top.

4.   Peel the garlic and crush into a bowl. Add the breadcrumbs, herb and oil and thoroughly blend together with a fork. Spoon evenly over the top of the tomatoes.

5.   Place in the hot oven and bake for about 20 minutes, or until the tomatoes are tender and the topping is crisp and golden brown.

MICROWAVE + GRILL

1.   *Put the tomatoes into a bowl and cover with boiling water. Leave to stand for 5 minutes, then drain, cut out the stem ends and slip off the skins. Lightly spray a shallow baking dish with oil.*

2.   *Cut the tomatoes into thick slices and arrange, slightly overlapping, in the baking dish. Sprinkle with salt and pepper and drizzle the vinegar over the top.*

3.   *Peel the garlic and crush into a bowl. Add the breadcrumbs, herb and oil and thoroughly blend together with a fork. Spoon evenly over the top of the tomatoes.*

4.   *Cook on MEDIUM-LOW+GRILL for about 10 minutes or until the tomatoes are tender and the top crisp and golden brown.*

BUTTERBEAN PURÉE

This smooth creamy purée goes well with grilled or roast meat or poultry or with a casserole. If I am cooking Aromatic Pork (page 138) and want to serve it with something more substantial than salad leaves, the Butterbean Purée is my choice.

Serves 2

Approximately 0.5g of fat per serving

1 small onion
1 garlic clove
400g can butterbeans
50ml/2 fl oz vegetable stock
1 tsp finely grated lemon rind
2 tsp lemon juice
1 tsp finely chopped fresh sage
freshly milled salt and black pepper

1. Peel the onion and garlic and chop finely. Drain the butterbeans, rinse under cold water, then drain again.

2. Put the onion, garlic and stock into a non-stick pan. Cover and cook over medium heat for 2-3 minutes or until soft.

3. Add the beans, cover and continue to cook for about 3 minutes or until the beans are very soft.

4. Mash to a rough purée with a potato masher.

5. Stir in the lemon rind and juice, the sage and seasoning to taste. Serve piping hot.

MUSHROOMS WITH GREMOLATA

The very large flat mushrooms have lots of flavour and cook quickly on a hot griddle, a fry-pan or under the grill. Topped with the combination of lemon, parsley and garlic (which the Italians call 'gremolata') and served on toast, they make a good light meal or a substantial starter. If you have some in the refrigerator, the toast can be spread with roasted garlic (page 201), with Tomato or Low Fat Pesto (pages 190 and 192) but the mushrooms are very juicy if you wish to leave it unadorned.

Serves 2   *Approximately 3g of fat per serving*
(served on plain toast)

1 garlic clove
3 tbsp finely chopped fresh parsley
finely grated rind of 1 small lemon
2 or 4 large flat mushrooms, depending on your appetite
2 large slices of granary bread
freshly milled salt and black pepper

1.   Peel the garlic and crush on to a small plate. Add the parsley and lemon rind and blend together with a fork. Trim the mushrooms and wipe with a dry tea-towel.

2.   Heat a griddle, non-stick fry-pan or a grill and add the mushrooms. Cook until golden brown, turning once.

3.   Meanwhile, toast the bread, place on warmed plates and, if using, spread with roasted garlic or pesto.

4.   Place the cooked mushrooms on top of the toast, drizzling over any pan juices. Add seasoning to taste and spoon the gremolata mixture over the top. Serve immediately.

5

FISH

LEMON AND MUSTARD CRUSTED HALIBUT

The simple lemon and mustard marinade flavours the fish and adds an appetising crust. I serve the fish with the Tomato Gratin (page 106) and some boiled potatoes sprinkled with chopped chives.

Halibut is a firm white fish; alternatively you could use cod, monkfish or Antarctic sea bass. Ask your fishmonger for his advice, they often have lesser-known fish which are well worth trying; ideally you need chunky boneless pieces of fish

Fish should only be marinated for up to thirty minutes, after that it starts to 'cook' from the acid ingredients in the marinade mixture. This recipe could be cooked on a barbecue.

Serves 2   *Approximately 7g of fat per serving*

1 garlic clove
2 tbsp lemon juice
1 tsp olive oil
1 tbsp wholegrain mustard
freshly milled salt and black pepper
2 chunky halibut steaks, about 175g/6 oz each
oil spray
lemon wedges, to serve

1. Peel and crush the garlic and place in a plastic bag with the lemon juice, oil, mustard and a good seasoning of salt and pepper.

2. Add the fish, gently turn to coat with the marinade, then refrigerate for 15-20 minutes.

3. Preheat a griddle or non-stick fry-pan and lightly spray with oil. Add the fish and cook over medium heat for about 4 minutes each side or until it flakes easily when tested with a fork. Serve with lemon wedges.

BAKED SEA BASS

You can use this simple way to cook whole fish using either one sea bass or two trout. You need about 450-550g/1-1¼ lb of fish in total for two servings.

Small new potatoes, quickly boiled in their skins and sprinkled with crushed sea salt, are the perfect partner to the rich fish.

Serves 2

Approximately 4g of fat per serving

1 sea bass or 2 sea trout, ready-to-cook, about 450g/1 lb total weight
4 spring onions
1 tbsp finely chopped or grated fresh ginger
3 tbsp finely chopped fresh coriander
1 tbsp soy sauce
1 tsp sesame oil
freshly milled salt and black pepper

1. Preheat the oven to 200°C/ gas mark 6. Cut a piece of foil large enough to wrap the fish loosely and place it on a baking tray.

2. Using a very sharp knife cut two or three diagonal slashes through the fish skin on both sides. Place the fish in the centre of the foil.

3.   Trim the spring onions and finely chop. Add to the ginger and coriander and stir to combine.

4.   Spread half the herb mixture inside the fish and the remainder over the top. Drizzle the soy sauce and oil over the top, plus a good seasoning of salt and pepper.

5.   Bring the sides of the foil together and fold to make a loose parcel. Twist the ends to seal.

6.   Place in the hot oven and bake for about 25 minutes or until the fish is cooked through.

7.   To serve: If serving sea bass, use a long sharp knife to remove the head (if there). Holding the knife horizontally cut along the backbone, then slide the knife under the flesh against the bones so that you can lift the whole side of the fish off the bones in one piece. Place on a warmed dinner plate. Carefully turn the fish over and repeat to remove the other side. Trout can be served whole or as above. Serve immediately.

BLACKENED FISH

'Blackened' is a term most usually associated with Cajun cooking. It doesn't mean something that is cooked to charcoal but a spice and herb coating sprinkled on to fish and poultry before cooking in a very hot pan to give the food a crisp crust. Cajun cooking is a tasty combination of French and southern American states cuisine with the emphasis on boldly flavoured spices. You will find various 'Cajun spice' mixtures amongst the regional foods in the stores but it is simple to make your own. Store in a tightly lidded jar and try it as a coating on meat, poultry and fish.

Choose thick cuts of white fish such as sea bream, bass or cod fillets or cod steaks.

Serve the fish with wedges of lemon or with crunchy cucumber, Sun-dried Tomato Sauce or Cucumber and Pickled Ginger Relish, all in Chapter 8.

This recipe could be cooked on the barbecue.

Serves 2

Approximately 2.5g of fat per serving

1 tsp ground cumin
2 tsp freshly milled salt and black pepper
1 tsp cayenne pepper
1 tsp turmeric
1 tsp freeze dried oregano
1 tsp paprika
1 tsp chilli powder
2 portions of fish – about 175g/6 oz each
oil spray
To serve: lemon wedges or sauce – see above

1. Place all the spices, seasoning and herbs into a small jar, cover tightly and shake to combine.

2. Lightly spray the fish with oil, then generously coat with the seasoning mixture.

3. Preheat a non-stick fry-pan, griddle pan or the barbecue.

4. When very hot, add the fish and cook until crisp and dark golden brown on the outside and opaque throughout. The actual cooking time will depend on the cut and thickness of the fish.

5. Serve piping hot.

FISH AND POTATO STEW

This is a richly flavoured and coloured combination of ingredients that makes you feel good even before you have eaten the first spoonful. I serve it in shallow bowls with spoons and forks and some warm crusty Ciabatta bread.

Concentrated fish stock is easy to find. Fish sauce is a pungent Asian ingredient made of salty fermented fish such as anchovies. It varies in strength depending on the manufacturer but the kind you will usually find in our supermarkets is a fairly mild clear liquid. It is quite salty so check before adding extra seasoning to the Stew. You will find fish sauce amongst the Oriental sauces in the stores. If you haven't any, use 1-2 tsp anchovy essence instead.

Serves 2

Approximately 8g of fat per serving

1 medium baking potato, about 175g/6 oz
1 small onion
1 small head of fennel
2 garlic cloves
115g/4 oz firm white fish such as cod or monkfish
250g can mussels in brine
oil spray
½ tsp turmeric
pinch fennel seeds
200g can chopped tomatoes
1 tbsp sun-dried tomato paste
600ml/1 pint fish stock
2 tbsp oriental fish sauce
50g/2 oz prawns, thawed if frozen
1 tbsp finely chopped fresh parsley
freshly milled salt and black pepper

1. Peel the potato and cut into small cubes. Peel and finely chop the onion. Trim the fennel and cut into thin wedges, reserving any green feathery leaves. Peel and crush the garlic. Remove any skin from the fish and cut into bite-sized pieces. Drain the mussels, rinse under cold water and dry on paper towel.

2. Heat a large non-stick pan (I use a wok) and lightly spray with oil. Add the potato, onion, garlic and fennel. Cook, stirring, over medium heat for 5 minutes. Stir in the turmeric and fennel seeds and cook for 1 minute.

3. Add the chopped tomatoes, tomato paste, stock and fish sauce. Stir well.

4. Bring just to the boil, then cover and cook over medium heat for about 10 minutes or until the potato and fennel are just tender. Add the fish and continue to cook for 3-4 minutes. Add the mussels, prawns and parsley and cook for 1-2 minutes or until the fish is just cooked through (it should be opaque).

5. Season to taste. If you have any green fennel leaves, finely chop, add to the parsley and sprinkle on top of the stew after ladling it in to warm shallow bowls.

FISH WITH A HERB AND LEMON CRUST

Gremolata is the classic Italian combination of finely chopped parsley, lemon rind and garlic which adds a colourful garnish to such dishes as Osso Bucco. With the addition of breadcrumbs and lemon juice, it makes a tasty crust for roasted fish steaks.

To serve with the fish I cut ripe tomatoes in half horizontally and place them, cut side-up, in a shallow baking dish. Lightly sprinkle with sugar and cook in the oven for the same time as the fish.

Choose thickly cut boneless white fish steaks such as cod or halibut or chunky pieces of monkfish.

Serves 2

Approximately 7g of fat per serving

1 lemon
1 garlic clove
25g/1 oz fresh white breadcrumbs
2 tbsp finely chopped fresh parsley
2 tbsp finely chopped fresh chives
2 tsp olive oil
freshly milled salt and black pepper
2 boneless thick white fish steaks, about 175g/6 oz
  each
2 tsp Dijon mustard
watercress sprigs for garnish

1. Preheat the oven to 200°C/gas mark 6.

2. Finely grate the rind and squeeze the juice of half the lemon. Cut the other piece in half to serve with the fish. Peel and crush the garlic.

3. Put the breadcrumbs, lemon rind and juice, garlic, herbs and oil into a bowl and add a good seasoning of salt and pepper. Mix with a fork until well blended.

4. Spread the mustard on all sides of the fish and coat with the breadcrumbs mixture, pressing it on with your fingers. Place the fish on a nonstick baking sheet slightly apart and pile any remaining crumbs on top.

5. Place in the hot oven and cook for 15-20 minutes or until the fish is cooked through and the breadcrumbs are golden brown and crisp.

6. Slip on to warmed plates and garnish with the watercress sprigs and reserved lemon wedges.

GINGERED PRAWNS WITH VEGETABLES

This dish is definitely one for a very relaxed casual meal so provide each eater with a small bowl of warm water and a pile of paper napkins, then it is in with the fingers. You will need to serve this recipe in bowls (with forks and spoons) as there is quite a lot of delicious broth and remember to have some hot crusty bread ready, too. If you are not happy about the informality, remove the prawn shells completely before cooking.

If you can't find raw prawns, use a 250g/8 oz bag of frozen cooked tiger prawns, making sure they are thoroughly thawed and dried on paper towel before using them. Add with the bean sprouts and cook until both sprouts and prawns are hot.

Serves 2

Approximately 2g of fat per serving

6 sun dried tomatoes (dry-packed, not in oil)
1 small red or yellow pepper
50g/2 oz button mushrooms
2 small courgettes
6 spring onions
225g/8 oz uncooked tiger (or large) prawns
410g can bean sprouts
1 tbsp finely chopped or grated fresh ginger
2 tbsp soy sauce
1 tbsp fish sauce
150ml/5 fl oz vegetable stock
freshly milled salt and black pepper

1. Cut the tomatoes in half (easiest with scissors) and place in a small bowl. Cover with boiling water and leave for 15 minutes. Cut the pepper in half lengthways, then remove and discard the stem, any white pith and the seeds. Cut the flesh into small squares. Trim the mushrooms, wipe with paper towel and cut in half or into thick slices, depending on the size. Trim the courgettes and onions and cut into thin slices. Peel the prawns leaving the tails on. Tip the bean sprouts into a strainer, rinse under cold water and leave to drain.

2. Drain the tomatoes and put into a wok. Add the vegetables, ginger, soy and fish sauces and the stock. Bring just to the boil, reduce the heat to low and cook for about 5 minutes or until the vegetables are just tender.

3. Add the prawns and bean sprouts and continue to cook for 2-3 minutes or until the prawns are completely opaque.

4. Season to taste, then ladle into large warmed bowls. Serve piping hot.

GRILLED TROUT WITH A SPICED COATING

Serve with only the simplest of vegetables, such as boiled potatoes sprinkled with finely chopped fresh parsley and sea salt. For the best results, the grill or griddle pan must be very hot before placing the fish under (or over) it so that it needs the minimum cooking time and remains succulent inside, crisp and golden brown outside. This may be cooked on the barbecue.

Serves 2   *Approximately 8g of fat per serving*

2 tbsp natural yogurt
1 tsp paprika
pinch ground cinnamon
pinch cayenne pepper
1 garlic clove
1 tsp olive oil
freshly milled salt and black pepper
2 ready-to-cook trout, about 175g/6 oz each
oil spray
lemon wedges to serve

1. At least one hour before cooking: Put the yogurt into a small bowl and add the paprika, cinnamon and cayenne pepper. Peel and crush the garlic and add with the olive oil and seasoning. Whisk to combine.

2. Cut deep diagonal slashes along each side of the fish at 2.5cm/1 in intervals. Rub the spiced yogurt over the skin and into the slashes on both sides. Cover and refrigerate for 1-2 hours.

3. Preheat the grill or griddle pan to very hot and lightly spray with oil before placing the fish on it.

4. Cook the fish for about 6 minutes, carefully turning it once, or until the skin is crisp and a rich golden brown and the fish is cooked through. Serve garnished with the lemon wedges.

MARINATED KIPPER FILLETS

The humble kipper fillet becomes an elegant dish when marinated in a vinegar and brown sugar mixture. To serve as a starter I line two small bowls with small crisp lettuce leaves and spoon the fish in the centre. Serve with fingers of unbuttered toast. For an easy meal, I add thinly sliced tomatoes, cucumber, some slender wedges of chicory and serve with warm granary bread.

Serves 4 as a starter   *approx. 6.5g of fat per serving*

Serves 2 as a main course   *approx. 13g of fat per serving*

225g/8 oz kipper fillets
1 small onion
1 small celery heart
75ml/2½ fl oz white wine vinegar
3 tbsp soft brown sugar
1 tbsp finely chopped fresh chives
freshly milled black pepper

1. At least 12 hours before serving: Carefully pull off the skin of the kippers and cut the flesh into very thin strips. Place in a non-metallic shallow dish.

2. Peel and very thinly slice the onion. Separate into rings and add to the fish.

3. Thinly slice the celery heart and add to the fish.

4. Mix the vinegar, sugar, chives and pepper to taste and spoon over the fish and vegetables. Cover and refrigerate for at least 12 hours, stirring once or twice.

5. Remove from the refrigerator 30 minutes before serving to allow the flavours to develop.

6. Serve as suggested above.

SALMON WITH A CITRUS AND SHERRY SAUCE

Although salmon has a higher fat content than most white fish, it is of the desired polyunsaturated type (Omega-3) and so is good for you. Salmon can be cooked in a wide variety of ways, in this recipe the marinade adds extra rich flavour and then later becomes a delicious sauce.

To serve with the grilled salmon, I like to cook 115g long grain white rice with 400ml vegetable stock, plus the finely grated rind and juice of one large lemon. (Cook to package directions using the stock and lemon in place of water.) At the end of the cooking time, I fold in some very finely shredded raw spinach (from a pack of baby spinach leaves), cover the dish and leave to stand while I cook the salmon. To serve, fluff up the rice with a fork and pile on warm plates. Place the salmon on top and drizzle the sauce around the plate. Very stylish!

The salmon could also be cooked on a barbecue or a griddle.

Serves 2

Approximately 18g of fat per serving

3 spring onions
1 lemon
1 garlic clove
2 tbsp orange juice
2 tbsp sweet sherry
2 tbsp soy sauce
2 tbsp maple syrup
2 thick salmon fillets, about 150g/5½ oz each

1. About 1 hour before cooking: Trim the spring onions and cut into thin slices. Halve the lemon and squeeze the juice from one half. Cut the other half into two pieces and set aside. Peel and crush the garlic.

2. Put the onions, lemon and orange juice, garlic, sherry, soy sauce and maple syrup into a shallow dish and stir together. Add the salmon and turn to coat it with the marinade. Cover and refrigerate for about 1 hour, turning occasionally.

3. Preheat the grill.

4. Remove the salmon from the dish with two forks, reserving the marinade, and place on a non-stick baking sheet.

5. Grill for about 5 minutes on each side or until the fish flakes easily when pierced with a fork.

6. Meanwhile, tip the remaining marinade into a small pan and bring to the boil. Allow to bubble for a minute or two until it has reduced and is slightly syrupy.

7. Pile the rice on to warmed plates, and add the salmon. Spoon over the sauce and serve garnished with the reserved lemon pieces.

SALMON WITH A COUSCOUS CRUST

The couscous makes a crunchy golden crust and keeps the salmon moist during cooking. Some crisply cooked green beans or sugar snap peas go well with this dish or try the Tomato and Red Onion Salad on page 188.

Although salmon has a high fat content, it is the right kind, the Omega 3 oil, which should be included regularly in our menus. Farmed salmon has a softer texture and milder flavour than wild salmon and is invariably the fish sold at a reasonable price in food stores. The fillet cut, which is boneless, is cut across the filleted side of the fish to give a neat serving portion. If you prefer, remove the skin before cooking.

Serves 2   *Approximately 22g of fat per serving*

25g/1 oz couscous
finely grated rind and juice of 1 large orange
1 tbsp whole grain mustard
1 tbsp fresh thyme leaves
freshly milled salt and black pepper
2 salmon fillets, about 175g/6 oz each

1. Preheat the oven to 200°C/gas mark 6. Place the couscous in a bowl and stir in 3 tbsp boiling water. Leave to stand for 10 minutes.

2. Stir in the orange rind, mustard and thyme and seasoning to taste.

3. Place the fish a little apart in a shallow ovenproof dish. Spoon the couscous on top and pour the orange juice round the fish.

4. Cook, uncovered, for 15-20 minutes or until the fish is cooked through.

5. Lift the salmon fillets on to warmed plates and spoon any couscous and juice in the dish around them.

SALMON WITH A FRESH GINGER SAUCE

I like to serve rice cooked in vegetable stock with this dish and, to add a delicious peppery taste, I add a handful of roughly chopped rocket or watercress to the hot rice just before serving and lightly stir in with a fork.

Serves 2　　　　　*Approximately 21g of fat per serving*

1 small onion
1 garlic clove
1 tbsp soft brown sugar
2 tbsp soy sauce
1 tbsp dry white vermouth
1 tbsp lemon juice
2 salmon fillets, about 175g/6 oz each
oil spray
2 tsp grated or finely chopped fresh root ginger
freshly milled salt and black pepper

1.　Peel the onion and finely chop. Peel and crush the garlic. Combine the garlic, sugar, soy sauce, vermouth and lemon juice in a small bowl.

2.　Cook the salmon in a non-stick frypan over medium-high heat for about 6 minutes, turning until golden brown on all sides and just cooked through. Remove to a warmed plate and lightly cover with foil.

3.　Lightly spray the hot pan with oil, add the onion and ginger and cook, stirring, until soft and brown.

4.　Add the garlic and soy mixture and bring just to the boil. Reduce the heat to low and return the salmon to the pan.

5.　Cook for a minute or two, turning the salmon to coat it with the glaze. Season to taste and serve.

SUMMER SALMON WITH CHIVE SAUCE

Definitely a dish for summer days, the golden salmon steaks look very appetising served with the creamy chive sauce, and the tiny new potatoes take on additional flavour when cooked in vegetable stock. Add a crisply cooked green vegetable such as slender green beans or sugar snap peas to complete the dish.

Be sure to buy real Greek yogurt (not Greek-style) to make this dish. Despite only containing 10g of fat per 100g it can be gently heated without separating (but do not allow it to boil). Be generous with the herbs, they taste delicious and look so pretty.

Serves 2

Approximately 18g of fat per serving

375g/13 oz tiny new potatoes
300ml/½ pint vegetable stock
2 salmon fillets, about 125g/4½ oz each
freshly milled salt and black pepper
4 tbsp dry white vermouth
1-2 tbsp finely chopped fresh chives
1-2 tbsp finely chopped fresh tarragon
4 tbsp Greek yogurt

1. Scrub the new potatoes (not to remove the skin but just any lingering soil) and place in a non-stick fry-pan with the stock.

2. Bring to the boil, then cover the pan and reduce the heat to a gentle simmer. Cook for 5 minutes or until almost tender, then uncover and continue to cook until the potatoes are cooked through and glazed with the stock.

3. Season the salmon with pepper on both sides. Heat a non-stick fry-pan and add the salmon. Cook over medium heat until cooked through, turning once. It will need 3-4 minutes each side. Remove from the pan and keep warm.

4. Off the heat, add the vermouth to the pan. Bring just to the boil, then reduce the heat to low and stir in the herbs and yogurt. Stir until the yogurt is just warmed through (do not allow to boil). Season to taste.

5. Spoon the potatoes onto warm plates, add the salmon and sauce and serve immediately.

TROUT PARCELS

Cooking fish in a parcel seals in all the flavours and aromas. Slide each parcel on to a warm plate, add the vegetables you are serving and open the parcel at the table to enjoy the wonderful aroma. I serve the trout with something simple such as rice or tiny new potatoes.

Foil could be used (but not in a microwave oven) in place of baking paper, however it doesn't look as attractive and you may need to cook the fish for a few minutes longer.

Serves 2

Approximately 4.5g of fat per serving

3 spring onions
2 small courgettes
1 tbsp finely chopped or grated fresh ginger
2 tbsp soy sauce
pinch of five spice powder
freshly milled black pepper
2 trout fillets, about 100g/4 oz each

1. Preheat the oven to 190°C/gas mark 5.

2. Cut two squares of greaseproof or non-stick baking paper, each approximately 35cm/14 in square.

3. Trim the spring onions and courgettes and cut into fairly thin slices. Whisk together the ginger, soy sauce, five spice powder and a good seasoning of pepper.

4. Place one trout fillet in the centre of one piece of paper, folding the thinner end under to make a compact shape. Top with half the spring onions and courgettes, then spoon over half the ginger mixture. Fold the paper over the fish and pleat the ends together to make a parcel. Carefully lift on to a baking sheet. Repeat with the other trout fillet.

5. Bake for 15-20 minutes or until the trout is just opaque and flakes easily.

6. Lift each parcel on to a warmed plate, open the top and serve immediately.

MICROWAVE METHOD (See page 215.)

Prepare as above, using greaseproof or non-stick baking paper. Place the parcels on a flat plate and cook on MEDIUM-HIGH for about 8 minutes or until the fish and vegetables are cooked.

6
MEAT

BEEF AND MUSHROOMS IN BLACK BEAN SAUCE

Rice, cooked in vegetable stock, is excellent with this dish. If you slip the piece of steak (or any meat or poultry you are stir-frying) into the freezer for an hour before cooking, you'll find it easier to cut into very thin slices

Serves 2   *Approximately 7g of fat per serving*

175g/6 oz fillet steak
1 green chilli
225g/8 oz button mushrooms
1 bunch spring onions
1 garlic clove
2 tbsp soy sauce
2 tbsp soft brown sugar
2 tbsp dry sherry
4 tbsp black bean sauce
oil spray
freshly milled salt and black pepper

1. Cut the steak into very thin slices. Cut the chilli in half lengthways, removing and discarding the stem and seeds. Cut into very fine slivers. (Wash your hands after preparing chillies as they can irritate the skin.) Trim the mushrooms and cut in half if large. Trim the onions and cut into 5cm/2 in lengths. Peel and crush the garlic. Measure the soy sauce, sugar, sherry and black bean sauce into a bowl and stir to combine.

2. Heat a non-stick wok and, when hot, lightly spray with oil. Add the slices of beef and cook over a high heat, stirring constantly, until well browned.

3. Add the chilli, mushrooms, onions and garlic and continue to cook, stirring, for 2-3 minutes.

4. Stir in the soy sauce mixture and cook until bubbling hot. Season to taste and serve immediately.

AROMATIC PORK

I have suggested serving Aromatic Pork with mixed salad leaves but, if I want something a little more substantial, I cook two portions of stir-fry noodles while the pork is in the pan, drain them well, then toss with the dressing. Another good alternative would be the Butterbean Purée on page 108.

Serves 2

Approximately 17.5g of fat per portion

1 small green chilli
4 tbsp finely chopped fresh coriander
1 garlic clove
finely grated rind and juice of 1 lemon
1 tbsp fish sauce
1 tbsp soy sauce
freshly ground salt and black pepper
350g/12 oz well-trimmed pork fillet
1 tsp clear honey
2 tsp olive oil
250g/8 oz bag ready-to-eat mixed salad leaves

1. Up to two hours before cooking: Halve the chilli, scoop out and discard the seeds and finely chop the flesh. Place HALF the chopped chilli and HALF the coriander in a small bowl, reserve the remainder. (Wash your hands after preparing chillies as they can irritate the skin.) Peel and crush the garlic and add to the bowl with HALF the lemon rind and juice and all the fish and soy sauce. Stir to combine and season with pepper.

2. Cut the pork into two portions, place slightly apart in a large plastic bag and flatten to an even thickness with a meat mallet or a rolling pin. Add the chilli, coriander and lemon mixture, secure the open end of the bag and gently shake to coat the meat with the marinade. Refrigerate for 1-2 hours, turning the bag over once.

3. To make the dressing: Put the remaining chilli, coriander, lemon rind and juice into a small bowl and add the honey, oil and a good seasoning of salt and pepper. Whisk to combine.

4. Preheat a non-stick griddle or frypan. Using a fork, lift the pork out of the marinade and place on the hot pan. Cook for 4-5 minutes per side or until golden brown and cooked through.

5. Tip the salad leaves into a bowl, add the dresssing and toss to combine. Pile on to serving plates, add the pork and serve immediately.

PORK WITH BLACK BEANS

The very lean cut of pork called the fillet or tenderloin has a relatively low fat content, is quick to cook and makes a delicious change from chicken. I serve this dish with rice (cook before starting to cook the stir-fry) or with noodles, which can be cooked at the same time as the stir-fry.

Five-spice powder is used frequently in Chinese cooking. It is a blend of five ground spices – cinnamon, cloves, fennel seed, star anise and Szechuan peppercorns. You will find it in all supermarkets. Remember it is easier to cut meat very thinly if it has been in the freezer for an hour before using.

Serves 2

Approximately 3g of fat per serving

225g/8 oz pork fillet
1 tsp cornflour
2 tsp soft brown sugar
2 tsp five-spice powder
225g/8 oz thin leeks
4 tbsp oyster sauce
3 tbsp black bean sauce
1-2 tsp chilli sauce
3 tbsp dry white vermouth or dry sherry
freshly milled black pepper
2 portions stir-fry rice noodles
oil spray

PORK WITH CHICKPEAS AND
PRESERVED LEMON

1. Up to 1 hour before serving: Trim any visible fat
    from the pork and, holding a sharp knife at a 45°
    angle, cut across into very thin slices. Place in a
    plastic bag and spoon in the cornflour, sugar and
    five-spice powder. Holding the open end closed,
    shake the bag to coat the meat evenly with the
    spiced flour. Refrigerate until needed.

2. Trim the leeks and cut into quarters lengthways.
    Rinse under cold running water to remove any grit,
    then drain well and cut into short lengths. Put the
    oyster, black bean and chilli sauces into a small
    bowl with the vermouth and a good seasoning of
    pepper. Stir to combine.

3. Cook the noodles to packet directions.

4. Heat a non-stick wok, lightly spray with oil and tip
    in the marinated pork. Cook over high heat, stirring
    constantly, for about 3 minutes or until the meat
    begins to brown (don't worry if it sticks slightly).
    Add the leeks and continue to cook over high heat,
    stirring constantly, for about 5 minutes until both
    pork and leeks are tender.

5. Drain the noodles and add to the wok.

6. Pour over the mixed sauces and cook, stirring
    (scrape up the browned bits on the bottom of the
    wok), just until bubbling hot. Serve immediately.

PORK WITH CHICKPEAS AND PRESERVED LEMON

This is really a complete meal in one pot but you could serve it with some rice or mashed potatoes. Alternatively, grill some Naan or pitta breads and use them to scoop up the delicious juices.

Preserved lemons are a fairly recent addition to the exotic food shelves in our stores and may be easier to find in a delicatessen. They originate from North Africa and the Middle East where they are used to flavour such dishes as both meat and poultry casseroles or vegetable couscous. To preserve them, the lemons are packed in salt and oil, and left until they are very soft. Preserved lemons will keep for about one week in the fridge and I have successfully frozen them. If you cannot find one, use a fresh lemon but first place it in a pan and cover with cold water. Bring just to the boil, then reduce the heat and allow to cook gently for 10 minutes. Cool and use as below.

Serves 2

Approximately 18g of fat per serving.

1 medium onion
2 garlic cloves
1 preserved lemon – see above
375g/13 oz lean pork fillet
1 tsp honey
1 tsp turmeric
200g can chopped tomatoes
300ml/½ pint chicken or vegetable stock
400g can chickpeas
freshly milled salt and black pepper

1. Peel the onion and cut into thin slices. Peel and crush the garlic. On a plate (to collect the juices) cut the lemon into thin wedges, discarding any seeds. Cut the pork into generous bite-sized pieces.

2. Put the onion and honey into a non-stick fry-pan. Cover and cook over medium heat, stirring once or twice, for about 5 minutes or until soft and golden brown. Stir in the turmeric.

3. Push the onion to one side of the pan and add the pieces of pork, stirring to coat them with the spice. Increase the heat and cook, stirring, until the pork has begun to brown.

4. Add the lemon wedges, tomatoes, stock and chick-peas. Stir to combine and bring just to the boil.

5. Cover the pan and reduce the heat to low. Gently cook for about 20 minutes or until the pork is very tender.

6. Season to taste before serving.

PORK WITH FRESH GINGER AND CHILLI

The secret of a successful stir-fry is taking the time to prepare the ingredients carefully, as the actual cooking time is so short. In fact, sometimes it takes longer to slice the meat or poultry and finely chop the vegetables than it does to cook them. It is far easier to slice meat and poultry very thinly if it is partly frozen. Either only partly thaw frozen items or slip fresh pieces into the freezer for about one hour before slicing. Look for pork fillet (also called tenderloin), which is labelled '90-95% fat free', as this will have been trimmed to remove every scrap of visible fat.

Serves 2

Approximately 3.5g of fat per serving

225g/8 oz pork fillet
2 tbsp soy sauce
1 tbsp dry white vermouth
2 medium-sized carrots
3 thin celery stalks
4 spring onions
1 clove garlic
1 fresh green chilli
1 tbsp very finely chopped or grated fresh root ginger
50ml/2 fl oz English apple juice
1 tsp honey
1 tsp cornflour
2 portions stir-fry rice noodles
freshly milled salt and black pepper

1. At least one hour before cooking: Using a very sharp knife held at a 45° angle, cut the pork into paper-thin slices. Spoon 1 tbsp soy sauce and the vermouth into a plastic bag and add the pork. Holding the open end shut, shake to coat the meat with the liquids. Refrigerate.

2. Peel the carrots, cut into matchstick sized pieces and put in a bowl. Trim and thinly slice the celery and spring onions. Peel and crush the garlic. Cut the chilli in half lengthwise, removing and discarding the stem and seeds. Cut the flesh into very fine shreds. (Wash your hands after preparing chillies as they can irritate the skin.) Add all the other vegetables to the carrots. Cover and refrigerate if not cooking immediately.

3. Just before cooking, whisk the apple juice, honey, cornflour and remaining soy sauce together.

4. To cook: Cook the rice noodles to package directions.

5. Preheat a non-stick wok. Tip in the pork and marinade and cook over high heat, stirring frequently until it is no longer pink. Add all the vegetables and continue to cook, stirring, for 2-3 minutes. Pour over the apple juice mixture and cook, stirring, until the carrots are just tender and the apple juice glaze has thickened.

6. Drain the noodles and add to the wok with seasoning to taste. Gently stir to combine, then spoon into warm bowls and serve immediately.

PORK TERIYAKI

To me, this is a summer recipe, to be enjoyed eating outside with a glass of chilled wine or beer and the pork kebabs cooking on the barbecue, but they will taste just as delicious cooked under the grill in the kitchen. I serve the pork and the cucumber relish with some warm soft floury baps and maybe with Tomato and Red Onion Salad (page 188) or simply sliced ripe tomatoes as well. Both the relish and the salad have delicious juices so bread is essential to mop them up.

When cutting meat to cook on skewers (kebabs) be sure to cut it in generous bite-sized pieces. The meat will shrink during cooking and, if the pieces are small, may end up rather dry and chewy after cooking. Ideally, the end result should be that the meat is well browned but still moist in the centre. Soaking wooden skewers prevents them burning during the grilling (or barbecuing) time.

Serves 2

Approximately 14g of fat per serving.

2 tbsp soy sauce
2 tbsp saké or dry sherry
1 tbsp clear honey
375g/13 oz lean pork fillet
½ a small pineapple
1 small cucumber (or ½ a large one)
freshly milled salt and black pepper
1 small red chilli
1 tbsp very finely chopped preserved ginger
2 tbsp rice wine vinegar
1 tbsp ginger syrup (from the jar of ginger)
leaves from 3-4 stems fresh mint, finely chopped

1. At least two hours before cooking: Combine the soy sauce, saké or sherry and the honey in a shallow non-metal dish. Cut the pork into generous bite-sized pieces and add to the marinade. Cut off both ends of the pineapple. Holding the fruit upright cut off the peel in vertical strips. Remove the eyes (the tiny small dark pieces) with the tip of a knife. Cut the fruit into chunks about the same size as the pork and add to the dish. Lightly stir the pork, pineapple and marinade together. Cover and leave to marinate in the refrigerator for at least two hours.

2. Cut the cucumber into very thin slices, spread on a plate and grind some salt over the top. Leave for 30 minutes. Rinse well under cold water, drain and dab with kitchen paper to remove as much moisture as possible. Place in a bowl. Cut the chilli in half, removing and discarding the stem and seeds. Very finely slice the flesh and add to the cucumber. (Wash your hands after preparing chillies as they can irritate the skin.) Mix the chopped ginger with the vinegar, ginger syrup and chopped mint. Add to the cucumber, toss well and season to taste. Chill until serving.

3. Soak 6 bamboo skewers in cold water for 20 minutes.

4. To cook: Preheat the grill or barbecue. Thread the pork and pineapple alternately on to the skewers. Grill for 8 minutes, turning frequently and basting with any remaining marinade, or until the pork is a rich golden brown.

5. Serve the skewers with the cucumber relish and warm bread.

GRIDDLED LAMB WITH BUTTERBEAN MASH AND GOLDEN ONIONS

Lamb neck fillet is a very sweet and tender cut of meat and needs only brief cooking so that the centre is still pink when served. I like to serve this dish with grilled Naan bread, the low fat version of course. If you are really hungry, use two cans of butterbeans to make the mash; alternatively replace the beans with mashed potatoes. The rich, golden brown, onion topping looks and tastes delicious and no-one would guess the onions were cooked without any fat.

The lamb could be cooked on a barbecue.

Serves 2

Approximately 23g of fat per serving

2 pieces of lamb neck fillet, about 225g/8 oz
1 lemon
1 tbsp sun-dried tomato paste
1 large onion
2 garlic cloves
2 tsp clear honey
400g can butterbeans
2 tbsp finely chopped fresh coriander or parsley
freshly milled salt and black pepper
2 low-fat Naan breads

1. Up to two hours before cooking: Place the pieces of lamb a little apart in a large plastic bag and slightly flatten to an even thickness with a meat mallet or rolling pin. Using a very sharp knife, make several deep cuts diagonally across each piece of meat. Cut the lemon in half and squeeze the juice of one half into a shallow dish. Stir in the tomato paste, add the meat and turn to coat evenly with the tomato mixture. Cover and leave in the refrigerator to marinate.

2.   Peel the onion, cut into thin slices and separate into rings. Peel the garlic.

3.   To cook: Put the onion into a large non-stick fry-pan and drizzle the honey over the top. Cook over medium heat for about 10 minutes, stirring once or twice, or until a rich dark brown. Remove from the heat and keep warm.

4.   Preheat a non-stick griddle pan. Add the lamb and cook over medium heat for about 10 minutes, turning the meat once, or until it is brown and crusty but still pink in the middle. Cover and keep warm.

5.   Drain the beans and put into a small pan. Cover with cold water and add the garlic. Warm over high heat until bubbling hot. Drain and mash with a potato masher or fork. Stir in the coriander or parsley and season to taste.

6.   Sprinkle the Naan bread with cold water and pop under a hot grill for 1 minute each side.

7.   Spoon the butterbean mash on to warmed plates. Cut the lamb into thick slices and arrange around the mash, then pile the onions on top. Cut the remaining lemon piece in half and add to the plates. Serve with the hot Naan bread.

MARINATED LAMB WITH HONEY AND THYME SAUCE

Serve with British new potatoes, broad beans no bigger than your thumb-nail and slim green beans. Choose well-trimmed chops that are at least 2.5cm/1 in thick.

Serves 2　　　　*Approximately 22.5g of fat per serving*

finely grated rind and juice of 1 large lemon
1 garlic clove, peeled and crushed
several sprigs of thyme
2 lean boneless lamb chops, about 225g/8 oz
2 tbsp white wine vinegar
1 tbsp clear honey
freshly milled salt and black pepper

1.　Up to two hours before cooking: Put half the lemon rind and juice into a shallow non-metallic dish. Add the garlic to the dish. Strip the leaves of thyme off their woody stalks and add half to the dish.

2.　Place the chops in the dish and turn to coat evenly with the lemon and herbs. Cover and refrigerate for up to two hours.

3.　Put the remaining lemon rind, juice and thyme leaves, the vinegar and honey into a small saucepan.

4.　To cook: Preheat a non-stick griddle, fry-pan or barbecue. Add the chops and cook over high heat until a rich, golden brown on both sides but still pink in the middle. This will be about 4 minutes on either side but does depend on the thickness of the meat. Cover and leave to stand for a minute or two (this allows the meat to 'relax').

5.　Bring the sauce ingredients to the boil and season to taste. Serve the chops on warmed plates with the sauce spooned over the top.

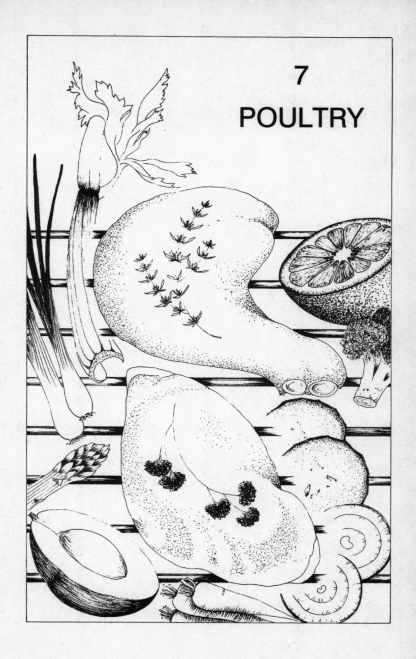

7
POULTRY

OVEN BAKED CHICKEN

Meaty chicken thighs marinated with herbs and lemon take on a rich flavour in this simple recipe. The marinade becomes the sauce in which the chicken cooks to a rich, crusty brown glazed finish. To save on washing up, line the roasting tin with foil before adding the chicken.

Utilise the oven space by cooking jacket potatoes or Oven Baked Rice (see page 58) at the same time.

Serves 2   *Approximately 8g of fat per serving*

4 large skinned chicken thighs
2 garlic cloves
finely grated rind and juice of 1 large lemon
2 tbsp fresh thyme leaves
2 tbsp clear honey
freshly milled salt and black pepper
lemon wedges, to serve

1. The day before: Place the chicken in a plastic bag. Peel and crush the garlic and add to the chicken with the lemon rind and juice, the thyme leaves and honey.

2. Holding the bag closed, shake to coat the chicken with the marinade. Place the bag in a bowl and refrigerate for up to 24 hours, turning over several times.

3. To cook: Preheat the oven to 190°C/gas mark 5.

4. Tip the chicken and marinade into a baking tin and arrange the chicken in a single layer. Sprinkle with salt and pepper.

5. Cook, uncovered, for 45 minutes, turning the chicken over once, or until it is cooked through and a rich dark brown. Serve with the lemon wedges.

POACHED CHICKEN WITH BABY VEGETABLES

The success of this dish depends on cooking over a low heat so that all the ingredients retain their shape; the stock should barely bubble once you have added the vegetables.

Poaching chicken on the bone adds extra flavour to the cooking liquid of which there is a generous amount. I serve the chicken and vegetables in shallow soup bowls with quite a lot of stock and provide each person with a spoon. Or you could serve a small bowl of stock, garnished with finely chopped parsley and chives, as a first course before the chicken. Alternatively, use the remaining stock as a base for a soup or as the liquid to cook rice. First, pour the stock through a sieve into a jug, refrigerate overnight and then remove any fat that may have hardened on the surface.

Serves 2

Approximately 6.5g of fat per serving

2 chicken breasts on the bone
1 lemon
8 baby new potatoes
3 celery stalks
6 baby carrots
4 small shallots or pickling onions
175g/6 oz asparagus spears or broccoli florets
600ml/1 pint chicken stock
4 tbsp dry white vermouth
4 black peppercorns
several sprigs of parsley
freshly milled salt and black pepper
1 tbsp finely chopped fresh tarragon

1. Remove and discard the skin and all visible fat from the chicken but leave the meat on the bone. Place the chicken in a large pan (I use a wok).

2. Using a swivel potato peeler, carefully cut two or three strips of the lemon peel, removing the yellow peel only. Add to the chicken. Squeeze the juice from the lemon and set aside. Scrub the potatoes. Trim and cut the celery into short lengths, reserving any leaves. Scrub and trim the carrots. Cover the shallots (or onions) with boiling water and leave to stand for 5 minutes. You will then be able to slip off the skins. Remove any woody ends from the asparagus and cut into bite-sized pieces (or cut the broccoli into bite-sized pieces).

3. Add the stock, vermouth, peppercorns and parsley to the chicken. Bring to the boil, then reduce the heat to low.

4. Add the potatoes, celery with any leaves, carrots and shallots (or onions). Cover and cook over low heat for 15 minutes.

5. Add the asparagus (or broccoli), cover and cook for a further 5 minutes or until the chicken and vegetables are tender.

6. Using two forks, lift the chicken on to a warm plate and carefully remove and discard the bones, keeping the meat in one piece. Place each piece of chicken on a warmed dinner plate and keep warm.

7. Using a slotted spoon remove the vegetables from the stock and arrange with the chicken.

8. Add a dash of lemon juice to the stock and season to taste. Spoon a little over each portion of chicken and sprinkle the tarragon over the top.

SPICED CHICKEN WITH DRIED FRUITS AND LEMON COUSCOUS

Chicken thighs gently cooked in a richly flavoured liquid become very tender with the meat just falling off the bone. This recipe has a generous amount of delicious sauce and the lemon couscous goes well with it. Alternatively, serve with rice or mashed potatoes.

Marsala is the Italian fortified wine which gives the dessert Zabaglione its distinctive taste. It has a rich almost smoky flavour and is excellent added to poultry dishes. If you prefer, a medium-sweet sherry could be used instead, giving a different flavour to the dish.

Serves 2

Approximately 12g of fat per serving

1 large onion
1 tbsp clear honey
1tsp ground cumin
1 tsp ground ginger
1 tsp turmeric
½ tsp ground cinnamon
4 large skinless chicken thighs
6 ready-to-eat prunes
6 ready-to-eat dried apricots
200ml/7 fl oz chicken stock
finely grated rind and juice of 1 large lemon
200ml/7 fl oz vegetable stock
115g/4 oz couscous
a generous dash of Marsala
freshly milled salt and black pepper

1. Peel the onion and cut into thin slices. Put into a non-stick fry-pan with the honey and cook over a medium heat, stirring frequently, until very soft and beginning to brown.

2. Stir in the spices and cook for a minute or two. Add the chicken thighs, turning to coat them with the spices. Increase the heat to high and cook, turning the chicken several times, until it is a rich golden brown.

3. Add the prunes, apricots and the chicken stock. Bring just to the boil, then cover and reduce the heat to low. Cook for about 25 minutes, turning the chicken once or twice, or until it is very tender when pierced with a fork.

4. Meanwhile, put the lemon rind and juice and the vegetable stock into a pan and bring to the boil. Remove from the heat and stir in the couscous. Cover and leave to stand for 5-10 minutes.

5. Using a fork, lift the chicken out of the fry-pan and keep warm. Add the Marsala to the pan and bring to the boil, scraping the sticky bits off the bottom of the pan. Bubble for a minute or two just to reduce the sauce slightly. Season to taste.

6. Fluff the couscous with a fork and pile on to two warm plates. Add the chicken and spoon the sauce over the top. Serve immediately.

SPICED CHICKEN AND VEGETABLES

We are all familiar with roast potatoes but other root vegetables are just as good; in fact, roasting brings out the natural sweetness of both carrots and parsnips.

Chicken thighs are an excellent and economical choice for this recipe which only leaves you with one baking pan to wash up (even less if you line the pan with foil before adding the chicken). If you can't find any very small onions, cut two medium-sized onions in half horizontally and place in the pan cut-side down. I use a mild flavoured curry paste but if you like a strong curry flavour, choose a hotter curry paste.

Serves 2

Approximately 13g of fat per serving

6 shallots or tiny pickling onions
2 medium carrots
2 small parsnips
2 medium-sized baking potatoes
4 large skinned and boned chicken thighs – about
    375g/13 oz
1 clove garlic
1 tbsp mild curry paste
1 tbsp clear honey
½ tsp turmeric
50ml/2 fl oz natural yogurt
1 tbsp mint jelly
¼ of a cucumber
freshly milled salt and black pepper

1. Preheat the oven to 180°C/gas mark 4. Cover the shallots or pickling onions with boiling water and leave to stand for 5 minutes, then drain and slip off the skins. Peel the carrots, parsnips and potatoes and cut into chunky even sized "chips". Cut each chicken thigh into three fingers.

2. Peel and crush the garlic into a medium bowl. Add the curry paste, honey and turmeric and stir together. Add the vegetables and chicken, and stir to evenly coat with the curry mixture.

3. Tip the chicken and vegetables into a shallow non-stick baking tin, scraping all the curry mixture on top of them. Arrange in a single layer.

4. Place in the hot oven and cook, uncovered, for 30 minutes or until the chicken and vegetables are tender, turning everything over halfway through the cooking time.

5. Just before serving, whisk the yogurt and mint jelly together. Cut the cucumber into quarters length-ways and scoop out the seeds. Finely chop the flesh and stir into the yogurt. Season to taste.

6. Spoon the chicken and vegetables on to warmed plates and drizzle the minted yogurt and cucumber over the top.

HARISSA CHICKEN WITH LEMON DHAL

This is a delicious fusion of African and Indian flavours with a dash of Oriental if you choose to include the optional Cucumber and Pickled Ginger Relish (on page 200). Harissa, that pungent Tunisian paste of chillies and spices, makes an instant marinade for the chicken breasts. The Dhal, the staple of Indian cookery, here has the addition of fresh lemon and coriander as well as the traditional spices. The optional relish, a simple combination of grated cucumber and Japanese pickled ginger, makes a cool contrast with the rich flavours of the other two items. If you are really hungry, add some low-fat Naan breads.

Serves 2

Approximately 9g of fat per serving

**2 skinned and boned chicken breasts, about
    150g/5½ oz each
finely grated rind and juice of 1 large lemon
1-2 tbsp harissa paste, to taste
1 medium onion
2 garlic cloves
1 tsp clear honey
1-2 tsp grated or finely chopped fresh ginger
1 tsp sweet chilli sauce
a pinch of turmeric
a pinch of ground cumin
115g/4 oz red lentils
600ml/1 pint vegetable stock
freshly milled salt and black pepper
a small handful of roughly chopped fresh coriander**

1. At least 30 minutes before cooking: Using a sharp knife, make several deep cuts in the skinned (smooth) side of the chicken breasts. In a shallow non-metallic dish, combine HALF the lemon rind and juice with the harissa paste. Add the chicken, rubbing the marinade into the cuts and turning to coat them on both sides. Cover and refrigerate for at least 30 minutes.

2. Peel the onion and finely chop. Peel and crush the garlic.

3. To make the Dhal: Put the onion and honey into a non-stick pan. Cover and cook over medium heat for about 5 minutes, or until very soft but just beginning to brown. Add the remaining lemon rind and juice, the ginger, chilli sauce and the spices. Continue to cook for 1-2 minutes longer. Add the lentils and stock and bring just to the boil. Turn the heat down to low, cover the pan and cook for 10-15 minutes, stirring once or twice, or until the lentils are very soft.

4. To cook the chicken: Heat a non-stick griddle or fry-pan, add the chicken, cut-side up, and cook over a medium-high heat for 5 minutes or until a rich golden brown. Turn the chicken over and continue to cook for about 5 minutes longer or until it is browned and no longer pink in the middle.

5. Beat the Dhal with a wooden spoon (or mash with a potato masher) until smooth, then season to taste and stir in HALF the chopped coriander.

6. Spoon the Dhal on to warmed plates, add the chicken and sprinkle the remaining coriander over the top. Pile the Relish, if serving, on one side of the plate.

CARAMELISED CHICKEN WITH PEPPERED COUSCOUS

During cooking, the simple marinade of marmalade and mustard caramelises to a rich brown finish on the chicken, at the same time forming the basis for the well-flavoured sauce. If wished, instead of the couscous, serve with mashed potatoes (omitting the tomatoes, pepper and spring onions).

Serves 2

Approximately 7g of fat per serving

2 tbsp orange marmalade, preferably fine cut
1 tbsp whole grain mustard
2 chicken breasts, skinned and boned, about
  150g/5½ oz each
finely grated rind and juice of 1 large lemon
6 pieces of sun-dried tomatoes (the dry-packed
  variety)
1 small yellow pepper
6 spring onions
200ml/7 fl oz vegetable stock
115g/4 oz couscous
150ml/5 fl oz orange juice
1 tsp white wine vinegar
freshly milled salt and black pepper

1. At least one hour before cooking: Combine the marmalade and mustard in a small bowl. Place the chicken skinned side up on a cutting board and, using a sharp knife, make several cuts two-thirds of the way through the chicken. Then place the chicken cut side up in a non-metallic dish and spread the marmalade mixture over the top. Sprinkle over the lemon juice and leave to marinate for at least 1 hour (if preparing more than 1 hour ahead, cover and chill).

2. To cook: Cover the sun-dried tomatoes with boiling water and leave to stand for 5 minutes. Quarter the pepper, discarding the stem, any pith and the seeds. Cut the flesh into small cubes. Thinly slice the spring onions. Drain the tomatoes and roughly slice.

3. Put the stock, pepper, spring onions and tomatoes into a saucepan and bring to the boil. Stir in the couscous. Remove from the heat, cover and leave to stand.

4. Heat a non-stick fry-pan. Using a fork, remove the chicken from the marinade and place, cut side down, in the hot pan. Cook over a moderately low heat for about 5 minutes, turn over and continue to cook for a further 5 minutes or until cooked through. Lift the chicken on to a warm plate, cover and keep warm.

5. Add the orange juice to the fry-pan and bring to the boil, stirring. Allow to boil for 2 minutes or until slightly reduced. Stir in the vinegar, then pour through a fine strainer into a jug. Season to taste.

6. Gently stir the couscous with a fork, spoon on to warm plates and place the chicken on top. Pour over the sauce and serve.

CHICKEN AND PASTA AU GRATIN

Tender chunks of chicken with pasta in a creamy sauce make a complete dish, needing just some crisp salad to add crunch to the meal.

Dry white vermouth can be used in place of wine, or use lemon juice.

A packet of skimmed milk powder is useful to have in the cupboard, not only when you forget to buy fresh milk but to add creaminess to sauces and soups with very little extra fat.

Serves 2

Approximately 12g of fat per serving

1 small onion
1 garlic clove
2 skinned and boned chicken breasts, about
     150g/5½ oz each
400ml/14 fl oz apple juice
3 tbsp dry white wine
125g/4½ oz small pasta shapes
3 tbsp dry skimmed milk powder
3 tsp cornflour
2-3 tsp mild mustard
freshly milled salt and black pepper
2 slices of bread
2 tsp olive oil

1. Peel the onion and garlic and cut both into quarters. Place in a shallow pan (a fry-pan is perfect), with the chicken, skinned side uppermost, the juice and wine.

2. Cover the pan and bring just to the boil. Reduce the heat to low and cook for 15-20 minutes or until the chicken springs back when pressed with a finger and is no longer pink in the centre. Remove the chicken and cut into bite-sized pieces.

3. Pour the stock through a strainer into a measuring jug. You should have about 300ml/½ pint.

4. Cook the pasta to packet directions. Drain thoroughly.

5. Add the milk powder and cornflour to the cooled stock and whisk until smooth. Pour into a pan, bring to the boil, then reduce the heat to medium and cook, stirring constantly, until smooth and thickened. Stir in the mustard (to taste) and seasoning.

6. Combine the chicken, pasta and sauce, and spoon into a shallow ovenproof dish.

7. Cut the bread into tiny cubes and toss with the oil until evenly combined. Scatter evenly over the pasta and chicken.

8. Place under a hot grill until the top is golden brown and crisp.

CHICKEN IN MANGO AND TAMARIND SAUCE

This is a richly flavoured dish combining tender chicken with a sweet-sour sauce and soft chunks of fresh mango. Rice, cooked in chicken stock, is the perfect partner.

Tamarind paste is a recent addition to the numerous flavourings now crowding our supermarket shelves. Made from the crushed fruit of a tree native to Asia, India, the West Indies and South America and widely used in dishes there, the paste has a sweet-sour, pungent, fruity taste and a rich dark colour. It can be used in salad dressings, particularly for bean or lentil salads (see the Lentil and Chicken Salad on page 76), marinades and curries.

Serves 2

Approximately 6g of fat per serving

1 mango
2 tbsp finely chopped or grated fresh root ginger
3 generous tsp tamarind paste
150ml/5 fl oz vegetable stock
1 large onion
2 skinned and boned chicken breasts, about
**   150g/5½ oz each**
oil spray
freshly milled salt and black pepper

1. Cut through the mango horizontally, as close to the flat stone on each side as possible. Carefully cut all the flesh from around the stone, peel and place in a blender or processor. Peel one of the halves, cut into chunks and add to the blender. Peel and cut the other half also into chunks and set aside.

2. Add the ginger, tamarind paste and stock to the blender and buzz until smooth.

3. Peel the onion and cut into thin slices. Separate into rings. Cut the chicken diagonally into finger-sized strips.

4. Heat a non-stick wok or fry-pan and lightly spray with oil. Add the onion and chicken, and cook over high heat, stirring constantly, until rich, golden brown.

5. Pour over the mango sauce and add the mango chunks. Reduce the heat to low and cook for about 5 minutes, stirring occasionally, or until the chicken is cooked through and the mango chunks softened.

6. Season to taste and serve.

CHICKEN WITH BALSAMIC VINEGAR AND ORANGE SAUCE

Rice cooked in chicken stock goes well with this dish. Just before serving, I may stir a good handful of chopped fresh chives to the hot rice, lightly stirring them in with a fork.

Slightly flattening the chicken to an even thickness reduces the cooking time needed. When you cook a piece of poultry or fish which has been boned, such as a chicken breast or a fillet of plaice, in a preheated pan, always place the boned side down on to the hot surface first. That surface of the chicken/fish will instantly contract forming an attractively shaped portion. If you had placed the food skinned-side down, it would have curled up.

Serves 2

Approximately 6g of fat per serving

2 tbsp balsamic vinegar
150ml/¼ pint orange juice
1 large orange
2 skinned and boned chicken breasts, about 140g/5 oz each
oil spray
several sprigs of fresh thyme
2 tsp clear honey
freshly milled salt and black pepper

1. Add the balsamic vinegar to the orange juice. Finely grate the rind of the orange and also add to the orange juice. Using a sharp knife, cut off all the white pith of the orange. Cut either side of the orange segments to remove them neatly and put them on to a plate.

2. Place the chicken breasts in a single layer in a large plastic bag. Using a meat mallet or a rolling pin, slightly flatten to an even thickness.

3. Preheat a non-stick fry-pan. Lightly spray the chicken with oil on both sides and place, boned-side down, in the hot pan. Cook for 2-3 minutes or until golden brown. Turn over and cook for 2-3 minutes, then turn over again.

4. Add the orange juice and vinegar mixture and the thyme. Bring just to the boil, then reduce the heat to low, cover and cook for about 5 minutes or until the chicken is cooked through.

5. Using a fork, lift the chicken on to warmed plates.

6. Add the honey to the pan and turn the heat to high. Allow the pan juices to bubble, stirring constantly, until they have reduced and thickened slightly. Remove from the heat, stir in the orange segments, season to taste and spoon over the chicken.

TURKEY STEAKS WITH CAPER SAUCE

I serve this dish with piping hot couscous, with a lot of finely chopped fresh mint forked through it. Alternatively, if I have a little more time, I make the Couscous Salad with Mint and Tomatoes on page 182. I know I am a fanatic about fresh herbs but oregano, to me, is the one herb, along with Herbes de Provence, that smells and tastes better dried. Buy it in very small amounts and use quickly before it loses its pungency.

Serves 2

Approximately 2.5g of fat per serving

1 tbsp plain flour
1 tbsp dried oregano
2 turkey breast fillets, about 150g/5½ oz each
1 lemon
1 large onion
2 garlic cloves
oil spray
300ml/½ pint chicken stock
25g/1 oz raisins
2 tbsp capers
freshly milled salt and black pepper

1. Combine the flour and oregano on a plate. Add the turkey steaks and coat with the flour, patting it on with the fingers. Thinly slice one half of the lemon and squeeze the juice from the remainder. Peel the onion, cut into thin slices and separate into rings. Peel and crush the garlic.

2. Heat a non-stick fry-pan and lightly spray with oil. Add the turkey steaks and cook over medium heat for about 5 minutes, turning once, or until golden brown on both sides. Remove from the pan and keep warm.

3. Add the onion to the pan and cook over medium heat for about 5 minutes, stirring once or twice, or until very soft.

4. Stir in the garlic, stock, lemon juice and raisins. Bring to the boil, scraping the browned bits from the bottom of the pan. Reduce the heat to medium and bubble the sauce for a minute or two until it has reduced slightly.

5. Return the turkey to the pan, cover and cook over low heat for 5 minutes or until the turkey is cooked through. Lift the turkey on to warmed plates.

6. Add the capers and seasoning to taste to the sauce and stir in. Spoon over the turkey and serve garnished with the lemon slices.

PAN FRIED TURKEY WITH APPLE

Low fat, low cost, tender and quick cooking – turkey breast steaks fulfil all those criteria. There is a generous amount of sauce so I would serve mashed or jacket potatoes or rice with this dish.

Serves 2

Approximately 6g of fat per serving

1 tbsp plain flour and 2 tbsp finely chopped fresh sage
freshly milled salt and black pepper
2 turkey breast steaks – about 150g/5½ oz each
1 small onion
2 celery sticks
1 red-skinned eating apple
oil spray
1 tsp walnut oil
300ml/½ pint English apple juice
1 tbsp Calvados or brandy, optional

1. Combine the flour, sage and a good seasoning of salt and pepper on a plate. Add the turkey steaks and coat with the herbed flour, rubbing it in to coat both sides.

2. Peel the onion and finely chop. Trim the celery and cut into thin slices. Cut the apple into eight wedges and remove the core.

3. Heat a non-stick fry-pan and lightly spray with oil. Add the turkey steaks and cook over high heat, turning once, until golden brown on both sides. Remove from the pan.

4. Add the walnut oil to the pan and swirl it around to coat the base. Add the apple wedges and cook over high heat, turning once, until golden brown. Remove from the pan.

5. Put the onion and celery into the pan and cook over medium heat, stirring, for a few minutes or until soft. Return the apple wedges to the pan, add the apple juice and Calvados or brandy, if using, and bring just to the boil.

6. Place the turkey steaks on top of the apple and cover the pan. Reduce the heat to low and cook for 10 minutes, turning the turkey once.

7. Lift the turkey steaks and apple wedges on to warmed plates and keep hot.

8. Turn the heat to high and bubble the sauce for a minute or two until slightly reduced in quantity. Season to taste, then spoon over the turkey and serve.

SPICED TURKEY STEAKS WITH MANGO AND RED ONION SALSA

Serve with hot rice cooked with chicken stock, piling the Salsa on top. If cooked on the barbecue, slip each steak inside a large soft bap, line with crisp lettuce leaves, and add a spoonful of Salsa. Marinating the steaks ensures they are tender when cooked.

Serves 2   *Approximately 3g of fat per serving*

6 tbsp low fat natural yogurt
2-3 tsp curry paste
2 turkey breast fillets, 150g/5½ oz each
1 small red onion
2 tbsp finely chopped fresh mint leaves
juice of ½ lemon
1 small ripe mango
freshly milled salt and black pepper

1. At least two hours before cooking or overnight: Place 3 tbsp of the yogurt into a small bowl, add the curry paste and whisk to combine. Put one turkey steak into a plastic bag and slightly flatten with a wooden meat mallet or with a rolling pin. Repeat with the second steak. Place the turkey on a plate, rub the yogurt mixture into both sides, then cover and refrigerate for at least two hours or overnight.

2. Make the Salsa just before serving: Peel and finely chop the onion and put into a bowl with the remaining yogurt, mint and lemon juice. Cut the mango into cubes as per step 1 on page 167. Add to the bowl. Stir and season to taste.

3. Place the turkey steaks under a preheated grill about 10cm/4 in from the heat and grill for about 5 minutes per side or until cooked through. Serve with the Salsa.

8

DRESSINGS
SALADS
SAUCES
&
RELISHES

HONEY AND MUSTARD DRESSING

The combination of apple juice, honey and wholegrain mustard makes a delicious salad dressing which goes well with all kinds of salad greens, as well as rice or pasta salads.

If you mix the dressing with a hand-held blender or in a processor, it will remain smooth and creamy when stored. If shaken in a jar, it may separate on standing so shake well again before using.

Makes about 160ml/5½ fl oz.

Use 2-3 tsp per serving.

Approximately 3-5g of fat per serving

150ml/5 fl oz apple juice
50ml/2 fl oz virgin olive oil
1 garlic clove, crushed
1 tbsp clear honey
1 tbsp whole grain mustard
freshly milled salt and black pepper to taste

1. Place all the ingredients into a screw-topped jar, the container for a hand-held blender or into a processor.

2. Shake, blend or process until the dressing is thoroughly combined.

3. To use, drizzle over a selection of salad ingredients and toss gently but thoroughly.

4. Store in a screw-topped jar at room temperature. Use within seven days.

SUN-DRIED TOMATO DRESSING

This salad dressing has a rich golden colour and lots of flavour. Use it to dress any kind of leaf, pasta or rice salad, or drizzle over hot new potatoes.

Makes about 300ml/½ pint

Approximately 5.5g of fat per 1½ tbsp

1 garlic clove
4 tbsp clear honey
4 tbsp olive oil
2 tbsp sun-dried tomato paste
5 tbsp red wine vinegar
50ml/2 fl oz English apple juice
freshly milled salt and black pepper to taste

1. Peel and crush the garlic.

2. Place all the ingredients in a screw-topped jar, the container for a hand-held blender or into a processor.

3. Shake, blend or process until the dressing is thoroughly combined.

4. Store in a screw-topped jar in the refrigerator. Use within seven days.

5. If mixed in a jar, it may separate on standing, so shake well again before using.

CORIANDER DRESSING WITH LIME

This simple low-fat dressing has many uses. Spoon over a well-flavoured piece of fish such as tuna just before serving; fork through freshly cooked rice to serve immediately with a curry dish or leave the rice to cool before adding other ingredients to make a rice salad; drizzle over a bowl of mixed salad leaves, toss and serve immediately.

Makes about 100ml/3½ fl oz

Use 2 tbsp per serving

Approximately 4.5g of fat per serving

2 tbsp rice wine or white wine vinegar
2 tbsp maple syrup
1 tbsp soy sauce
1 tbsp olive oil
finely grated rind and juice of 1 lime
chopped fresh coriander
freshly milled salt and black pepper to taste

1. Heat the vinegar and maple syrup just to the boil, then reduce the heat and bubble until syrupy.

2. Stir in the soy sauce and cool.

3. Add the lime rind and juice, the coriander and seasoning to taste.

4. Store in a screw-topped jar in the refrigerator. Use within three days.

MINT AND LEMON DRESSING

This is a good all-purpose salad dressing to dress any kind of salad, both rice and pasta, as well as leaves and vegetables. Refrigerated, it will be fresh for up to seven days.

When a salad dressing is made with a hand-held blender or in a processor, it becomes very creamy and remains so when stored. Dressings made in a jar tend to separate and will need to be given a good shake before each use to combine the ingredients together again.

Makes about 100ml/3½ fl oz

Use 2-3 tsp per serving

Approximately 4.5-7g of fat per serving

2 garlic cloves
75ml/2½ fl oz English apple juice
finely grated rind and juice of 1 large lemon
3 tbsp virgin olive oil
1 tbsp clear honey
freshly milled salt and black pepper
3 tbsp finely chopped fresh mint

1. Peel and crush the garlic.

2. Put the garlic, apple juice, lemon rind and juice, oil and honey into a screw-topped jar, the container of a hand-held blender or into a processor.

3. Shake, blend or process until the dressing is thoroughly combined.

4. Pour into a storage container and stir in seasoning to taste and the mint.

5. Store in the refrigerator for up to seven days.

ORANGE AND FRESH GINGER DRESSING

This salad dressing is full of rich flavours but just one tablespoon of oil. It will keep for up to a week in the refrigerator so it is worth making a double amount. As well as dressing a mixed green salad, it would add lots of flavour to a rice or grain salad.

You could substitute fresh orange juice for the frozen concentrate but the flavour will be milder. Chopped root ginger is now available in handy small jars ready for use but it is mixed with oil, so will increase the fat content of the dressing slightly.

Makes 150ml/5 fl oz

Use 1 tbsp per serving

Approximately 1.5g of fat per serving

**75ml/2½ fl oz (½ a can) frozen orange juice
concentrate, thawed
finely grated rind and juice of 1 lemon
1 tbsp finely chopped or grated fresh root ginger
1 tbsp clear honey
1 tbsp Dijon mustard
1 tbsp olive oil
1 tbsp soy sauce
1 garlic clove
freshly milled salt and black pepper to taste**

1. Place all the ingredients in a screw-topped jar, the container for a hand-held blender or a processor.

2. Shake, blend or process until the dressing is thoroughly combined.

3. Store, covered, in the refrigerator for up to one week.

COUSCOUS SALAD WITH MINT AND TOMATOES

There is very little cooking with this couscous salad and it makes a good complete meal served with some warm rolls. Make it about one hour before you want to eat it, to allow the flavour of the dressing to blend in with the other ingredients. It would also be good with the Turkey Steaks with Caper Sauce (page 170).

The mint jelly in the dressing is the kind you buy in a jar to serve with roast lamb. You will find it among the bottled sauces in the store. It adds an intense minty flavour to other recipes such as the sauce with Smoked Trout Kedgeree (page 72) and the Cauliflower and Lentil Curry (page 92). The rocket is optional but does add a bright peppery touch to the salad; watercress would be a good substitute.

Serves 2

Approximately 9g of fat per serving

225ml/8 fl oz vegetable stock
115g/4 oz couscous
3 spring onions
8 cherry tomatoes
1 tbsp raspberry or red wine vinegar
1 tbsp olive or walnut oil
1 tbsp mint jelly
freshly milled salt and black pepper
a handful of roughly chopped rocket leaves,
**   optional**

1. Bring the stock to the boil in a pan, add the couscous, cover and leave to stand for 5 minutes.

2. Trim the spring onions and cut into thin slices. Halve the tomatoes.

3. Put the vinegar, oil and mint jelly into a serving bowl. Whisk to combine, adding seasoning to taste.

4. Add the couscous and spring onions and gently stir together. Leave to cool to room temperature.

5. Just before serving check the seasoning and stir in the tomatoes and rocket.

MICROWAVE METHOD (See page 215.)

Put the couscous and HOT stock into a casserole and cook, uncovered, on HIGH for 4 minutes. Cover and leave to stand for 5 minutes. Complete the recipe as above.

GRILLED VEGETABLE AND BEAN SALAD WITH SUN-DRIED TOMATO DRESSING

This colourful combination of vegetables and beans makes a very satisfying meal when served with some crusty bread or a baked potato.

The flavours are at their best when the salad is served at room temperature. If chilling half the salad to serve the next day, remove from the refrigerator about one hour before you plan to serve it.

Serves 4

Approximately 9.5g of fat per serving

1 medium-sized aubergine
4 large plum tomatoes
1 large red onion
1 yellow pepper
1 orange pepper
8 cloves garlic
oil spray
2 tbsp clear honey
2 tbsp walnut or toasted sesame oil
1 tbsp sun-dried tomato paste
2 tbsp red wine vinegar
2 tbsp apple or orange juice
freshly milled salt and black pepper
400g can barlotti beans

1. Cut the aubergine into 2.5cm/1 in slices, discarding the stem. Cut the tomatoes into half lengthways. Peel the onion and cut into thick slices. Cut the peppers in half through the stem, discarding the stem, seeds and any white pith. Cut the flesh into thick fingers.

2. Arrange all the vegetables, including the garlic, in a grill pan. Lightly spray with oil and grill for 8-10 minutes, turning once, or until golden brown and soft.

3. Put the honey, oil, tomato paste, vinegar and apple or orange juice into a screw-topped jar and shake until thoroughly combined. Season to taste.

4. Tip the beans and their liquid into a pan and bring to the boil. Cook for 1-2 minutes until piping hot, then pour through a strainer to remove all the liquid. Place the beans in a shallow serving bowl.

5. Squeeze the garlic from its papery skin and add to the beans, stirring to combine. Add the vegetables and spoon over the dressing. Gently stir to coat all the vegetables and beans evenly with the dressing.

6. Serve at room temperature.

RADISH AND ORANGE SALAD

This crisp and crunchy salad goes well with strongly flavoured dishes such as Pork with Chickpeas and Preserved Lemon (page 142) or Caramelised Chicken with Peppered Couscous (page 162) where a light green-leafed salad would be overwhelmed by the other flavours.

Serve very soon after preparing so that the ingredients remain crisp.

Serves 2   *Approximately 5g of fat per serving*

finely grated rind and juice of ½ a lemon
1 tsp clear honey
a pinch of ground cinnamon
2 tsp olive oil
1 large orange
1 bunch of radishes
1 small red onion
2-3 sprigs of fresh mint
freshly milled salt and black pepper

1. Put the lemon rind, juice, honey, cinnamon and oil into a medium-sized salad bowl and whisk until well combined.

2. Remove the skin and white pith from the orange and, holding the fruit over the bowl, cut between the membrane to remove the segments of flesh, allowing the fruit to drop into the bowl.

3. Trim the radishes and cut into very thin slices (easiest on the slicing blade of a grater). Peel the onion, cut in half from stem to root end, then across into thin half-moon slices. Remove the mint leaves from the stems and roughly chop.

4. Add the radishes, onion and mint to the bowl. Toss to combine, adding seasoning to taste.

CARROT SALAD

Butterhead lettuce is the easily recognised (though not usually named) loose-leaf English lettuce available all the year round. The leaves are very tender and will bruise easily if used in a tossed salad. However, they are the ideal shape and size for lining an individual dish or bowl and filling with Carrot Salad, or with a potato or a prawn salad.

Serves 2

Approximately 8g of fat per serving

1 garlic clove
50ml/2 fl oz English apple juice
3 tbsp sherry vinegar
1 tsp clear honey
1 tbsp olive oil
1 tsp Dijon mustard
freshly milled salt and black pepper
225g/8 oz young carrots
25g/1 oz raisins
1 small Butterhead lettuce

1. Peel the garlic and crush into a medium-sized bowl. Add the apple juice, vinegar, honey, oil and mustard and whisk until combined. Season to taste.

2. Peel the carrots and grate coarsely. Add to the dressing with the raisins and, using two forks, toss lightly just to combine.

3. Break the lettuce gently apart into individual leaves. Arrange around the sides of two shallow bowls and spoon the carrots into the centre.

TOMATO AND RED ONION SALAD

I often serve this dish as a relish or salsa as well as a salad, it really fits all three descriptions. It goes well with grilled meats or fish, and with grain salads, such as couscous or rice. Try it with Salmon with a Couscous Crust (page 128) or Pork Teriyaki (page 146).

If you can find some yellow as well as red cherry tomatoes, use a combination of both. Only the appearance will change, the flavour will be the same.

Serves 2

Negligible fat content

250g/8 oz cherry tomatoes
1 medium sized red onion
1 garlic clove
1 tbsp fresh thyme leaves
1 tsp clear honey
2 tbsp red wine vinegar
freshly milled salt and black pepper

1. Up to two hours before serving: Cut each tomato in half, removing and discarding the stems. Place in a serving bowl. Peel the red onion, cut into very thin slices and separate into rings. Add to the tomatoes.

2. Peel and crush the garlic into a small bowl. Add the thyme leaves, honey, vinegar and a good seasoning of salt and pepper. Whisk to combine, then spoon over the tomatoes.

3. Gently stir together, then cover and leave at room temperature for 1-2 hours to marinate, stirring occasionally.

VERSATILE YOGURT

If you strain yogurt for several hours, it becomes thick and creamy rather like real Greek yogurt. It can be stirred into soups, sauces or curries just before serving to give a really creamy finish. Seasoned with salt and freshly milled black pepper plus finely chopped fresh herbs, it makes a very fresh tasting cream salad dressing – spoon over lettuce wedges, sliced tomatoes or chopped cucumber. Thin with a little orange or apple juice, whisk in some roasted garlic (see page 201) and use for a tossed salad. Sweeten the strained yogurt with honey or maple syrup or whisk in real vanilla extract and serve with fruit.

If you strain the yogurt overnight, it becomes very thick and smooth. Turn into a bowl, stir in seasoning and herbs and serve as a cheese with salad, use as a sandwich filling or in recipes. Cut into wedges and place on individual plates with a fruit garnish such as orange segments or ripe figs. Sift a little icing sugar plus cinnamon or cocoa powder over the cheese and serve as a very stylish dessert.

A nylon strainer will do the job but you can also buy very inexpensive purpose-designed re-usable yogurt strainers. They have a very fine nylon mesh so do not need to be lined with butter muslin.

Made with whole milk yogurt   *18g of fat*

Made with low-fat yogurt   *4.8g of fat*

600ml/1 pint natural yogurt, not a variety containing gelatine
seasoning or flavouring – see above

1.   Place a nylon strainer over a measuring jug and line with a piece of butter muslin. Tip in the yogurt.

3.   Refrigerate for several hours or overnight.

4.   Add seasoning or flavouring as wished.

TOMATO PESTO

Delicious though it is, the conventional recipe for pesto is heavy with pinenuts, Parmesan cheese and oil, making it a very high fat sauce, which is very difficult to use in a restrained way! I have reduced the fat count in my version on page 192 but this red pesto, with the concentrated flavour of sun-dried tomatoes, is even lower so that you can use it with more abandon.

A jar of this tucked away in the fridge has many uses. Spoon on to toasted slices of French bread for a quick snack or appetiser. Add a dollop to soups such as the Butterbean and Lemon (page 26) or the White Bean and Cabbage on page 24. Stir into fat-free crème fraiche and generously spoon on top of a steaming hot baked potato, or on top of a vegetable chilli. Serve as a colourful instant sauce with grilled or poached chicken or fish. For a quick snack, spread a split roll with Yogurt Cheese (page 189), add a generous layer of Tomato Pesto and a few lettuce leaves and enjoy.

The exact amount of herbs is not important, if unsure err on the generous side. As a rough guide, 25g/1 oz of basil is the leaves from a large supermarket pot or a generous handful from the garden. Ditto the chives. When herbs are plentiful, make in bulk, pack into small jars and freeze.

Makes about 200g/7 oz

Approximately 3.5g of fat per tablespoon

75g/2¾ oz dry-packed sun-dried tomatoes (not in oil)
2 garlic cloves
25g/1 oz chives
25g/1 oz basil leaves
25g/1 oz blanched almonds
2 tbsp olive oil
1 tbsp white wine vinegar
freshly milled salt and black pepper

1. Place the dried tomatoes and garlic in a bowl and cover with boiling water. Roughly chop the chives.

2. Drain the dried tomatoes and, using your fingers, squeeze out as much moisture as you can. (Discard the water.) Slice the garlic.

3. Put the almonds into a blender or processor and buzz just until finely chopped. Add the drained tomatoes, the herbs, garlic, oil and vinegar. Buzz in short bursts to a coarse texture. Take care not to over-process, you are aiming for an interesting finely-chopped texture, not a super-smooth sauce.

4. Season to taste, then spoon into a storage jar with a well-sealed lid.

5. Store in the refrigerator and use within two weeks (or freeze).

PESTO

Bought pesto contains around 5g of fat per measured tablespoonful and, if you are like me and somewhat addicted to the pungent flavour, it is very easy to use far more than that. So I just had to try and reduce the fat content without sacrificing any flavour.

Instead of using Parmesan cheese I use Pecorino, the Italian ewe's milk cheese, which has a pronounced strong salty flavour, and replaced the traditional pine nuts with walnuts, toasted first to bring out their flavour. As well as the traditional basil, I have used lots of parsley and chives, and added a little wine vinegar. The result is a brilliant green chunky-textured sauce, full of fresh herb flavour.

I make this pesto in bulk when fresh herbs are abundant, pack it in small jars and freeze to use in the winter. If I have lemon handy, I add the finely grated rind with the herbs and substitute lemon juice for the vinegar to make Lemon Pesto.

Add to hot pasta, rice or couscous. Swirl into low fat fromage frais and spoon on top of a baked potato. Toast thin slices of a baguette on both sides, spread with pesto and top with cooked shrimps for a pretty nibble.

Makes about 550g/1¼ lb

Approximately 4g of fat per tablespoon

55g/2 oz walnuts
115g/4 oz fresh parsley
115g/4 oz fresh chives
55g/2 oz Pecorino cheese
4 cloves garlic
115g/4 oz fresh basil leaves
75ml/2½ fl oz olive oil
2 tbsp white wine vinegar
freshly milled salt and black pepper

1. Spread the walnuts in a single layer in a non-stick fry-pan and cook over low heat, stirring frequently, until golden brown. Tip on to paper towel to cool.

2. Remove only the very thick stems of the parsley and rinse the herb in cold water. Roll in a tea-towel to remove all the water. Using scissors, roughly cut the chives. Cut the Pecorino into cubes. Peel the garlic.

3. Put the cheese into a processor and buzz to rough crumbs. Add the walnuts, garlic and all the herbs and buzz until roughly chopped. Do not over process as you are aiming for a chunky texture not a smooth purée. Add the oil and vinegar and buzz just to combine. Season to taste.

4. Spoon into a jar with a tight-fitting lid and store in the refrigerator or freezer. It will keep up to two weeks in the fridge, several months in the freezer.

FRESH GREEN HERB SAUCE

This vibrantly coloured and flavoured combination of herbs can be used in a multitude of ways. Serve as a sauce with poached or grilled fish and poultry, either just as it is or swirled into natural yogurt or low-fat fromage frais; add a spoonful or so to piping hot cauliflower florets or tiny new potatoes and gently toss to combine; whisk an extra spoonful of vinegar into two or three of sauce, check the seasoning and use to dress a green salad; swirl a spoonful into homemade or canned tomato soup; or just stir into freshly cooked rice or pasta or hot beans as an instant sauce.

Make it when herbs are abundant and cheap, spoon into small containers and store in the freezer to add a taste of summer to dishes in the winter. The exact amount of herbs is not important, I have given you a guideline but if you have plenty, be generous with the amount.

Makes about 150g/5½ oz

Use 1-2 tbsp per serving

Approximately 3.2g of fat per serving

1 large bunch flat-leaf parsley
10 sprigs basil
5 sprigs mint
1 bunch of chives
2 garlic cloves
1 tbsp capers packed in brine
4 small gerkins
1 tbsp oriental fish sauce or 2 tsp anchovy paste
1 tsp Dijon mustard
1 tbsp olive oil
1 tbsp rice wine or white wine vinegar
freshly milled salt and black pepper

1. Rinse the herbs under cold running water to remove any grit, drain and roll in a tea-towel so that you remove the moisture. Break off any thick parsley and basil stems. (Leave some thinner parsley stems as they contain a lot of flavour.) Pull the mint leaves off their stems. Peel the garlic and cut into thin slices. Rinse and drain the capers. Slice the gerkins.

2. Put the herbs, garlic, capers and gerkins into a processor and buzz just until roughly chopped, scraping down the sides of the bowl as needed.

3. Add the fish sauce, mustard, oil and vinegar and buzz briefly to combine.

4. Tip into a bowl and season to taste with salt, if needed, and pepper.

5. To store: Spoon into a screw-topped jar and keep in the refrigerator. Use freezer boxes if freezing.

SUN-DRIED TOMATO SAUCE

This is a useful sauce to have in the fridge (can be stored for up to a week) or freezer, to serve with pasta, rice or couscous, as a filling for a jacket potato or as a sauce for vegetables, such as cauliflower, with poached fish or chicken. For the best flavour, add the herbs just before reheating the basic sauce. When fresh herbs are not to hand, I use the frozen variety.

4 generous servings   *Approx. 3g of fat per serving*

115g/4 oz sun-dried tomatoes
600ml/1 pint boiling water
1 large onion
2 garlic cloves
2 tsp olive oil
juice of 1 lemon
2 tbsp finely chopped fresh parsley
2 tbsp finely torn fresh basil
freshly milled salt and black pepper

1. Soak the tomatoes in the water for 15 minutes.

2. Peel the onion and finely chop. Peel and crush the garlic. Put the oil into a non-stick pan with the onion and cook over low heat, stirring, until very soft.

3. With a fork, lift out one-third of the tomatoes and set aside.

4. Spoon the remaining tomatoes and their water into a processor or blender and buzz until smooth. Add to the pan with the reserved tomatoes.

5. Bring just to the boil, cover and cook over a low heat for 10 minutes. Stir in the lemon juice, herbs and seasoning just before serving.

CHILLI-PEPPER SALSA

Serve this colourful mixture with grilled chicken or fish as a crunchy salad garnish. Or spread toasted French bread slices with roasted garlic (see page 201), pile the Salsa on top and serve as a starter.

Makes 300ml, about 4 servings.

Negligible grams of fat per serving

½ **small red pepper**
7.5cm/3 in cucumber
2 spring onions
1 garlic clove
1 tbsp red wine vinegar
2 tsp chilli sauce
1 tsp clear honey
4 tbsp drained canned corn
freshly milled salt and black pepper

1. Remove and discard any pith and seeds in the pepper, then cut the flesh into small cubes. Halve the cucumber lengthways and scoop out the seeds. Cut the flesh into small cubes. Trim the onions and cut into thin slices.

2. Peel and crush the garlic into a medium bowl. Add the vinegar, chilli sauce and honey, and whisk to combine.

3. Stir in the pepper, cucumber, onions, corn and seasoning to taste.

4. The Salsa will keep, covered, in the refrigerator, for up to two days.

ONION RELISH

Another very useful item to have in the refrigerator to round out a simple meal, this Onion Relish will keep for 2-3 days. It goes well with cold meats or cheese and there is plenty of delicious sauce to mop up with crusty bread. The Relish can also be served warm, freshly made, with a grilled steak or pork chop.

For this recipe, I use small pearl onions, fresh pickling onions or the mild pink-skinned variety of shallot.

Serves 4

Approximately 4g of fat per serving

450g/1 lb onions (see above)
1 lemon
1 tbsp olive oil
3 tbsp dry white vermouth
3 tbsp tomato purée
3 tbsp clear honey
50g/2 oz raisins
freshly milled salt and black pepper
3 tbsp finely chopped fresh parsley

1. Put the onions into a bowl and cover with boiling water. Leave to stand for about 5 minutes, then drain, trim the root ends and slip off the skins. Dry on a tea-towel. Cut the lemon into thin slices, discarding any pips.

2. Put the onions into a non-stick pan and add the lemon slices, oil, vermouth, tomato purée, honey, raisins and 100ml/3½ fl oz cold water.

3. Bring just to the boil over medium heat. Stir well, cover and reduce the heat to low. Cook for 10-15 minutes (depending on the size of the onions), stirring occasionally, or until the onions are tender when pierced with the tip of a knife.

4. Using a perforated spoon, lift the onions and lemon slices into a serving bowl.

5. Bring the pan juices to the boil and cook over high heat for about 5 minutes or until they have reduced by half. Season to taste and pour over the onions. Cool, then cover and refrigerate if serving cold.

6. Serve sprinkled with finely chopped fresh parsley.

MICROWAVE METHOD (See page 215.)

1. *Put the onions into a bowl and cover with boiling water. Leave to stand for about 5 minutes, then drain, trim the root ends and slip off the skins. Dry on a tea-towel. Cut the lemon into thin slices, discarding any pips.*

2. *Put the onions, lemon slices, oil, vermouth, tomato purée, honey, raisins, and 100ml/3½ fl oz cold water into a casserole.*

3. *Cover and cook on HIGH for about 10 minutes, stirring once or twice, or until the onions are tender when pierced with the tip of a knife.*

4. *Using a perforated spoon, lift the onions and lemon slices into a serving bowl.*

5. *Cook the juices in the casserole on HIGH until they are reduced by half. Season to taste and pour over the onions.*

6. *Serve sprinkled with finely chopped fresh parsley.*

CUCUMBER AND PICKLED GINGER RELISH

This quick-to-make crisp relish, with Oriental overtones, goes well with any spicy food (try it with Harissa Chicken on page 160 or Caramelised Chicken on page 162) where it will add a cool contrast of flavour.

Pickled ginger is sliced or chopped fresh root ginger which has been preserved in sweet vinegar. A relative newcomer to our food stores, it is now readily available due to Japanese sushi, with which it is served as a garnish, also being sold here ready to eat at home. You will find it in sealed packets with the sushi display or in jars with the Oriental foods. It has a mild warm flavour. Add it to clear soups, stir into hot noodles or rice, or try some added to a chicken sandwich or salad.

Serves 2   *Negligible grams of fat per serving*

½ a cucumber
freshly milled salt and pepper
several pieces of pickled ginger, to taste
2-3 tsp rice wine or white wine vinegar

1. Ahead of time: Grate the cucumber on the coarse blade of a cheese grater and spread out on a large plate. Sprinkle generously with salt and leave for about 30 minutes.

2. Tip into a colander and rinse under cold water to remove the salt, then drain well. Spread on a dry tea-towel and blot to remove the moisture, then place in a shallow bowl.

3. Cut the ginger into slivers and add to the cucumber with the vinegar. Season with pepper and toss with two forks to combine. Taste and add more ginger if wished.

4. Serve immediately.

ROASTED GARLIC

When garlic has been roasted, it takes on a sweeter, mellow flavour and the flesh softens to a smooth purée. The cooked garlic can be spread on to toasted bread, forked into the middle of a jacket potato or used in recipes. If you find the taste of uncooked garlic rather overpowering, especially in recipes that do not need cooking, such as salad dressing, try using roast garlic.

Heat the oven to 160°C/gas mark 2. Break a head of garlic into separate cloves, place them on a square of foil and loosely gather the corners to make a parcel. Cook for about 40 minutes or until the cloves feel quite soft when pinched. Use the garlic immediately or loosen the foil to allow the steam to escape and the garlic to become cold. To store, close the foil and keep in the refrigerator (for up to two weeks).

Negligible fat content.

9
DESSERTS

GINGERED DATES

I love the rich smooth sweetness of dates and add them to sweet and savoury recipes. I add thinly sliced apple wedges and slivered dates to shredded Cos or Romaine lettuce and toss it with Orange and Fresh Ginger Dressing. About twenty minutes before a lamb or pork casserole is fully cooked, I often stir in a handful of whole dates.

Do make this recipe with dates from the familiar oval-ended long box, the larger fresh variety from Israel or, best of all, the even larger Medjool dates from California or Egypt. Do not use the dates sold for baking.

Serves 2

Negligible fat

8-12 dates depending on size
2 tbsp sweet sherry
1 tsp syrup from a jar of stem ginger
1 small knob stem ginger
75ml/2½ fl oz virtually fat free fromage frais

1. About 3 hours before serving: Remove the stones and quarter the dates. Place in a shallow dish and drizzle over the sherry and ginger syrup. Marinate for about three hours, stirring once.

2. Spoon the dates and marinade into individual dessert glasses. Finely chop the stem ginger and fold into the fromage frais. Spoon on top of the dates and serve.

RED FRUIT COMPOTE WITH TOASTED BRIOCHE

This dessert is second cousin to the traditional Summer Pudding but far simpler. The contrast of the chilled fruits and the hot sugared bread is delicious.

The compote needs no cooking just marinating in the refrigerator overnight. This quantity makes four servings but, in place of the brioche, the fruit is also delicious served with lemon sorbet, frozen vanilla yogurt or fat-free crème fraiche. Brioche loaves are easy to find in the supermarkets or you could use a slice of Pannetone, that wonderfully perfumed bread from Italy sold in pretty boxes, or just a light fruit bread from any baker.

Serves 4

Compote approximately 1g of fat per serving

Brioche approximately 4g of fat per serving

450g pack frozen mixed summer fruits
2 tbsp clear honey
1-2 tbsp brandy or Cointreau
2 thick slices of brioche
2 tsp caster sugar

1. The day before serving: Tip the fruit into a pretty serving bowl and drizzle the honey and the brandy or Cointreau over the top. Cover and refrigerate.

2. To serve: Gently stir the fruit.

3. Place the slices of brioche under a hot grill and lightly toast on both sides. Sprinkle the sugar evenly on one side of each slice and grill until golden brown.

4. Place each slice of brioche on a dessert plate and spoon the compote on top. Serve immediately.

GROWNUP JELLIES

Far removed from childhood teas, this is jelly with a subtle kick. Made of real fruit juice with a little additional flavouring, this jelly is very lightly set so that it quivers on the spoon. Serve in tall elegant glasses to enhance the colour.

Choose from the wide variety of real fruit juices to be found in the chilled section of the stores and match it to a compatible alcohol such as vodka with a citrus juice, Cointreau with orange or red berry juice, Crème de Framboise with a strawberry based juice, Crème de Cassis with a raspberry one. If wished, add a suitable fresh fruit garnish or just a sprig of mint just before serving.

Serves 4   *Negligible fat content*

600ml/1 pint real fruit juice
1 tbsp unflavoured powdered gelatine
3 tbsp chosen alcohol

1. Measure 6 tbsp of the juice into a small bowl and sprinkle the gelatine on top. Leave to stand for 5 minutes to allow the gelatine to soak up the juice. Place the bowl over a pan of gently simmering water and stir until completely dissolved (if you use a metal spoon you will be able to see when all the granules have dissolved).

2. Pour the rest of the juice into a jug and stir in the gelatine and alcohol.

3. Carefully pour into four tall glasses and refrigerate until set – about 4 hours. If you are chilling them overnight, cover each glass with clingfilm.

MICROWAVE METHOD (See page 215.)

Melt the gelatine in the microwave on MEDIUM/50% for about 1 minute. Do not allow to boil.

ORANGE AND STRAWBERRY COMPOTE

This is a pretty mixture of fruits to make when, if ever, you get tired of eating just plain strawberries.

Serves 2

Negligible fat

2 large oranges
300ml/½ pint fresh orange juice
3 tbsp clear honey
4 whole cloves
1 cinnamon stick
115g/4 oz small fresh strawberries

1. Using a swivel potato peeler, remove just the brightly coloured zest of half an orange (be sure not to remove any of the bitter white pith). Cut the zest into very fine shreds, place in a bowl and cover with boiling water.

2. Using a sharp knife, remove all the orange peel (including all the white pith) from both oranges. Holding the fruit over a serving bowl to catch any juice, cut into the centre of the fruit either side of each segment to remove the orange flesh. Allow the orange segments to drop into the bowl.

3. Drain the shreds of orange zest and put into a non-stick pan with the orange juice, honey, cloves and cinnamon. Gently heat to dissolve the honey. Leave to cool.

4. Add the strawberries to the oranges, pour over the orange syrup and gently stir. Chill before serving.

CARAMELISED FIGS WITH GINGERED FROMAGE

This is the dish to make when figs are plump and ripe. Serve piping hot, fresh from the grill, so that the hot fruit contrasts with the icy cool fromage frais. The hot figs would also be excellent served with lemon sorbet.

Serves 2

Negligible fat

6 tbsp fat-free fromage frais
1 piece of preserved ginger, finely chopped
2 tsp ginger syrup (from the jar)
6 fresh ripe figs
finely grated rind and juice of 1 lemon
2 tbsp soft, dark brown sugar

1. Place the fromage frais in a small bowl and stir in the ginger and syrup. Chill.

2. Cut the figs in half through the stems and place, cut-side up, in a shallow, flameproof dish.

3. Combine the lemon rind, juice and sugar and spoon over the figs.

4. Place under a preheated grill close to the heat source and cook for about 5 minutes or until the topping has melted and the figs begin to brown around the edges – keep an eye on them.

5. Spoon into bowls, drizzling any pan juices over the top, and serve with the fromage frais.

BAKED BANANAS WITH MAPLE CREAM DIPPING SAUCE

Bananas are a great, fresh convenience food already wrapped and ready to go! Delicious whenever you want to eat them, they are also excellent baked and served piping hot with this creamy sauce. They are at their best eaten freshly cooked – I put them in the hot oven just before serving the main course. I like to serve the sauce in small individual bowls placed on the same plate as the banana. You can then dip each slice of fruit into it before eating.

Only pure maple syrup has the intensity of flavour that is so delicious. Cheaper products are diluted with a less expensive flavourless syrup, such as corn syrup, or may even just have maple flavouring in them. Once opened, keep pure maple syrup refrigerated.

Serves 2   *Negligible fat*

2-3 tbsp pure maple syrup
125ml/4 fl oz virtually fat-free fromage frais
2 large firm bananas

1. Put the maple syrup and fromage frais in a bowl and whisk until combined. Refrigerate.

2. Preheat the oven to 180°C/gas mark 4.

3. Put the unpeeled bananas on to a baking sheet and bake for about 20 minutes, turning over once. When ready to eat they will feel hot, be totally black and very soft when gently pinched.

4. Spoon the sauce into two small bowls.

5. Place each cooked banana on a dessert plate, cut across the stem end and peel back the top part of the skin to expose the soft melting fruit inside. Serve immediately with the sauce.

BALSAMIC STRAWBERRIES

Strawberries and vinegar may sound an odd combination but this is a very special vinegar. Balsamic vinegar is made in Italy and for many years knowledgeable cooks could only buy it by taking an Italian holiday. Now you will find several varieties in the stores to select from and, like so many things, the more you pay the better the product. The vinegar gets its distinctive dark colour and mellow sweetness from many years of ageing in oak barrels. Small, very sweet strawberries can be served just sprinkled with balsamic vinegar straight from the bottle.

Serves 2

Negligible fat

3 tbsp balsamic vinegar
1 tbsp clear honey
225g/8 oz strawberries
lemon or strawberry sorbet or frozen yogurt

1. Measure the vinegar and honey into a small, non-stick pan and gently heat just to dissolve the honey. Do not allow to boil.

2. Hull and thinly slice the strawberries, reserving four whole for the garnish.

3. Arrange the sliced fruits on two dessert plates and top with a scoop of sorbet or frozen yogurt.

4. Drizzle the vinegar syrup around the fruit, add the reserved whole fruit and serve immediately.

MULLED FRUITS

With the flavour and aroma of hot, spiced wine this is a good dessert to serve on a chilly day when fresh fruit is unappealing. This recipe makes four generous servings. It can be gently reheated the second day but I serve it warm with one or two Amaretti di Saronno biscuits (made in Italy and wrapped in pairs in crisp tissue paper) the first day and the next day chilled with a spoonful of low fat crème fraiche or yogurt.

Serves 4

Negligible fat

115g/4 oz raisins
115g/4 oz ready-to-eat dried figs
115g/4 oz clear honey
150ml/¼ pint sweet red vermouth
2 cinnamon sticks
6 whole cloves
2 tsp grated root ginger
450g/1 lb pack frozen fruits of the forest or mixed fruits

1. Put the dried fruits, honey, vermouth, spices and ginger into a non-stick pan.

2. Cook, stirring constantly, over a medium heat until the honey and vermouth are just beginning to bubble.

3. Add the frozen fruits, reduce the heat to low and cook, stirring, until the fruits have thawed. Stir gently to prevent the fruits being crushed.

4. Continue to cook over low heat until the fruits are very warm.

5. Cover and leave to stand for 1-2 hours to allow the fruits to plump up. Gently reheat if serving warm.

6. Remove the cinnamon sticks and cloves before serving. Serve warm or chilled.

MICROWAVE METHOD (See page 215.)

1. Put the dried fruits, honey, vermouth, spices and ginger into a casserole.

2. Cover and cook on HIGH for 2 minutes.

3. Add the frozen fruits and cook, covered, on MEDIUM, for 2-3 minutes. Stir gently.

4. Cook, covered, on MEDIUM for 2-3 minutes or until the fruits are very warm.

5. Cover and leave to stand for 1-2 hours to allow the fruits to plump up. Gently reheat if serving warm.

6. Remove the cinnamon sticks and cloves before serving. Serve warm or chilled.

MICROWAVE COOKING

The microwave cooking times given are for 800-1000 watt models. For lower wattage models, cook a little longer; for higher wattage models, reduce the cooking time slightly, then check the result. All cooking is on HIGH unless otherwise stated. MEDIUM-HIGH is equivalent to 500-600 watts; MEDIUM to 350-400 watts; MED-LOW to 200-300 watts and LOW to 100-200 watts.

INDEX

Gingered Dates, 205

R
Radish and Orange Salad, 186
Red Cabbage with Pears, 104
Red Fruit Compote with Toasted Brioche, 206
Red Pepper and Sun-Dried Tomato Sauce, 53

Relishes:
Chilli-Pepper Salsa, 197
Cucumber and Pickled Ginger Relish, 200
Onion Relish, 198

Rice:
Rice and Black-Eye Beans, 62
Rice, Oven Baked, 58
Rice with Garden Vegetables, 64
Smoked Trout Kedgeree, 72
Spiced Basmati Rice, 60

Roasted Garlic, 201
Roasted Onions, 87

S
Salad:
Aubergine Salad and Chicken Wraps, 90
Bulgar Wheat Salad, 70
Carrot Salad, 187
Couscous Salad with Mint and Tomatoes, 182
Lentil and Chicken Salad, 76
Pasta and Chickpea Salad, 34
Potato Salad, Crunchy, 103
Potato Salad, Spiced, 103

Radish and Orange Salad, 186
Tomato and Red Onion, 188
Vegetable and Bean Salad with Sun-Dried Tomato Dressing, Grilled, 184

Salad Dressings:
Coriander with Lime, 179
Honey and Mustard, 177
Mint and Lemon, 180
Orange and Fresh Ginger, 181
Sun-Dried Tomato Sauce, 196

Salmon with a Citrus and Sherry Sauce, 126
Salmon with a Couscous Crust, 128
Salmon with a Fresh Ginger Sauce, 129
Salmon with Chive Sauce, Summer, 130

Sauces:
Herb Sauce, Fresh Green, 94
Pesto, 192
Red Pepper and Sun-Dried Tomato Sauce, 53
Tomato Pesto, 190
Tomato Salsa, 28
Tomato Sauce, Fresh, 52
Tomato Sauce, Red Pepper and Sun Dried, 53
Tuna and Lemon Sauce, 54
Very Quick Pasta Sauces, 52

Sea Bass, Baked, 114
Smoked Trout Kedgeree, 72

Soups:
Butterbean and Lemon Soup, 26